Panic to Peace

Living Free from the Grip of Fear

Dr. Neil McLamb

Copyright © 2016 by Neil McLamb
All Rights Reserved. Except as permitted under the U.S. Copyright Act of 1976, no part of this publication may be reproduced, distributed, or transmitted in any form or by any means, or stored in a database or retrieval system, without prior written consent of the publisher.

Scripture Taken from The Holy Bible, English Standard Version® (ESV®)
Copyright © 2001 by Crossway,
a publishing ministry of Good News Publishers.
All rights reserved.
ESV Text Edition: 2007

Cover Design by Kevin Keller
Edited by Ryan Goodrich
First Edition: February 2016

ISBN-13: 978-1523644568
ISBN-10: 1523644567

CONTENTS

AUTHOR'S NOTE ... i

LIVING IN FEAR

1) What is Wrong with Me? *Panic* ... 1
2) The Valedictorian Speech *End to Perfection* ... 7
3) Open House *A New Identity* ... 17
4) The Back Row *The Sweet Spot* ... 27
5) Skipping Class *Pressing Snooze* ... 37
6) Building Rome in a Day *Driven to Perform* ... 47
7) Snowball Effect *Living in a Fog* ... 55

UNMASKING THE PROBLEM

8) The Search *A Maze of Medicine* ... 63
9) Church Ain't Jiffy Lube *Surrender* ... 71
10) Someone Trustworthy *The Power of Acceptance* ... 79

BREAKING THE GRIP

11) Sunday Message *Unexpected Validation* ... 89
12) The Superstore *Fear from a New Perspective* ... 99
13) Another Speech *Focus on the Truth* ... 109

LIVING FREE: THE FINAL PIECE

14) More Than a Mind Game *No Fear in Love* ... 119
15) Warning Signs *Imperfection and Prayer Closets* ... 129
16) True Peace *A Father's Affection* ... 141

AFTERWARD ... 151
ACKNOWLEDGEMENTS ... 153
ABOUT THE AUTHOR ... 155

Author's Note

This book contains a story I have wanted to put into writing for a while. It is a true account of several years of my life. At times, I have shared pieces of it with others, as I have seen them struggling in their own ways and hoped something in my own story might connect with them and be helpful. I have had many opportunities to do that, and I am thankful for those moments. Sharing our stories with each other is an avenue by which God seems to enjoy engaging us.

This book may seem, in the beginning, like it focuses only on a struggle with panic attacks and extreme anxiety. Despite the fact that I would have thought the same thing several years ago, that perception could not be farther from the truth. There is much more to it.

In addition to telling about a time in my life in which fear was intertwined with everything I said, thought, and did, this book also tells the incredible story of how God revealed Himself to me in the midst of my fear. At my lowest point, I had no idea what the roots of my anxiety and fear really were. He intervened and showed me what was really going on. In that process, He taught me the most important truths I have ever known.

The journey in *Panic to Peace* begins with specific incidents that reveal how fear crept in and took over my life. From there, it moves to the in depth search for a solution. After the roots of the problem are uncovered, the story moves on to how fear was overcome, one step at a time. Finally, the concluding chapters reveal the foundation for moving forward in freedom and experiencing peace.

At the end of it all I knew God better than I did at the beginning, and I trusted Him more because of it. What I learned and experienced was vital to my freedom from panic and anxiety.

Those truths also served to set me free from other bondage I was in unknowingly.

Whether you are currently fighting to survive panic attacks, grinding out days haunted by anxiety and its horrid symptoms, scared to face something in your life that has left you paralyzed, stressed to the hilt with an overly busy life, in a current state of hopelessness, or loving someone struggling with those things, perhaps God will use my story to provide some hope and direction you need.

(1)

What is Wrong with Me?

*W*HAT IS HAPPENING? *Oh God, I feel sick.* I shake my head, trying to shrug off whatever is happening. It's not working. *I've felt "off" for the last few hours. Now that I think about it, I have been distracted with a very uneasy sensation the entire evening.* Whatever "it" is, it's been getting progressively worse since I first noticed the overall strange feeling while sitting in the restaurant earlier. *Could this be vertigo?* It sort of feels that way. My head feels ready to start spinning uncontrollably at any moment. But I've had vertigo before, and this feels… different. Whatever is going on, something bad is about to happen at any moment.

What is wrong with me? Something is wrong. I rub my head nervously. Since the start of the evening, I have been trying to fight through whatever this is. Up until now, I have been successful in hiding it from everyone and getting through the night.

I pull the car up under the shelter to the trailer that is home to my wife, my son, and me. I glance over at my good friend, Lavelle, who is seated in the passenger seat. Both our wives are in the back of the car, but they, like Lavelle, are all covered in a strange haze. Things look...different, almost as if I were detached from myself, watching events unfold from behind a television screen. Nothing feels real to me.

Maybe something I ate just isn't sitting well. I think for a second before discarding the thought. *I felt the sensation of this event coming on before I had even eaten a bite. That realization scares me even more. If it's not food poisoning, what the heck is it?*

After exiting the car, the feeling of detachment becomes even more pronounced. My conscious self keeps sending commands to my physical self to take each step, but the delay between feels excruciatingly long. I make it as far as the entryway before I realize fully that something is wrong. I sprint for the bathroom, and finally give up hiding it. My legs feel like they're stuck in mud as I take each step, and I call out for help.

"Melissa! Something is wrong! I think I am going to pass out or something!" I struggle to even get the words out, their meaning muddled behind an audible slur. "Am I having a stroke?"

I lean over the toilet, trying to make myself throw up. After several struggling attempts that leave me gagging, I cannot make myself vomit.

We've left Lavelle and Kelly in the den. I know they can tell something is wrong. An unshakable feeling of shame overtakes me, and I really wish they were not here for this embarrassing event. It makes me worry even more. What could they be thinking about me?

"I bet they think I'm crazy," I mumble, voice muffled by the close proximity of the toilet bowl to my face.

"They don't think you're crazy," Melissa says. "They are just worried."

I want to believe her, but I don't. They definitely think I'm crazy, and they may be right! My mind now races back and forth between wrestling with the pain and imagining that my friends are thinking I'm some kind of nutcase. The thought of them seeing me this way seems to fuel the turmoil inside of me. My failure to keep this hidden from them now adds shame to everything else weighing down my mind.

As if in answer to my mental decision, I am overtaken by an all-new pain that causes me to forget my obsession with what they think. God help me! I grab my chest, trying to push back the physical pain I suddenly feel inside. A surging flame of agony from inside rages, threatening to tear out of me.

"This feels like a heart attack!" I gasp through the overwhelming sensations. But I don't want to go to a hospital; the thought of going there is beyond terrifying and the humiliation all the more public.

I just need to get this under control... I shake my head vigorously, trying to shrug off the heavy weight that seemed to settle on me further. *I don't want to go to the hospital.* I fear what they might find wrong with me. Many possibilities run through my mind: stroke, heart attack, aneurysm…

Melissa tries to console me, rubbing my back as I crouch in front of the toilet. Despite my stationary location, the room is spinning violently and uncontrollably. My head feels like it weighs 100 pounds. I am so hot, I feel like crawling out of my own skin. I grit my teeth and ball up my fists. The harder I fight, the worse it seems to get. Although I am in full-on self-defense mode, it's like I'm taking blind swings at something in the dark. I'm not connecting with anything, and nothing I do is helping. I am in a freefall, scrambling to grab ahold of something on the way down to stop me. But there is nothing to grab, and there is nothing to catch me.

❖ PANIC ❖

That evening in 2004 was a real-life nightmare for me. I had been struggling with episodes like that for a few months. Until then, they had all occurred at night. I would go to sleep, like normal, only to awaken several hours later, completely unable to breathe. When I was forced out of sleep by the attacks, I would immediately jump out of bed and leave the bedroom so my wife wouldn't hear. I'd pace the hallway or walk outside for some fresh air until the event passed. I would do whatever I could to get through the nights. The one thing I could not do was lie there and relax. I did not want to admit it, the attacks were getting worse. And to my horror, they had invaded my daytime hours.

Although I did not know it, the episodes that I was having were full-blown panic attacks.

I became convinced that God was punishing me. I was keenly aware of my mistakes. I knew He knew about them. I also was convinced I wasn't doing enough to please Him and gain forgiveness for my shortcomings. It just made sense to me that He must have grown tired of watching me screw up and disappoint Him.

Panic attacks, debilitating anxiety, and fear; they all hit me like a ton of bricks, seemingly out of nowhere. But those things were not out of nowhere. I just thought they were at the time. Actually, there were hidden things in my life that I never would have suspected as the culprit.

This is the story of my journey through anxiety, panic, and fear, and, ultimately of my finding peace after suffering from the control they had over my life. To begin this journey, Chapter 2 travels back years before the panic attack described above occurred. Sharing a few pivotal moments from my past will help explain how I got to the point that I finally panicked. From that point on, you will be able to follow along with my story as my fears are faced, disempowered, and overcome. My hope and prayer is that through reading and sharing in my experiences, God might further encourage and empower you as you walk with Him through whatever you might be struggling with.

THINGS TO THINK ABOUT

1) Do you ever wonder what is happening in your own life or why you feel the way you do?

_____
_____

2) Symptoms of anxiety are numerous and different for everyone. Do you ever have symptoms of anxiety, such as shakiness, lightheadedness, dizziness, dry mouth, trouble sleeping, constant worry, trouble breathing, or stomach issues? Symptoms of panic attacks can vary as well. Have you ever had an episode similar to what I described?

_____
_____

3) Fear is something everyone deals with on some level. Has fear ever overwhelmed you? Has it ever caused you to avoid or do something you normally would not?

_____
_____

4) Do you ever feel like God is angry with you or punishing you? Do you ever feel like you have not done enough for Him?

_____
_____
_____

(2)

The Valedictorian Speech

THE YEAR IS 1992, SEVERAL WEEKS AFTER MY 14TH BIRTHDAY. I am graduating from the 8th grade, a significant milestone in my life. I've been at this same small school in North Carolina since Kindergarten. During those nine years, I've discovered I have the innate ability to do well in school. My report cards contain only "A's" and "S's." The A's, of course, are given for the different subjects taught each year. The S's are the grades issued for "Satisfactory Behavior." Information has always been easy for me to retain, and likewise I test well. I never cause problems in class, but rather I tend naturally toward being obedient and respectful. I guess you could say I am viewed by my parents, peers, and teachers as a smart, well-behaved young boy.

For many years, I've accepted and settled into this identity with no small level of contentedness. However, on this particular night, as I sit beside one of my teachers and in front of all my classmates, their families, and others, I question the intelligence of being such a great student. Until I was asked to speak at this event, I never thought about what being at the top of my class would inevitably require. A member of the County Board of Education smiles at me reassuringly as she gets up to read her speech, and then the realization of what is happening to me settles in.

I am the valedictorian of my 8th grade class. And, in just a few minutes, I have to get up in front of hundreds of people and deliver the speech my mother and I prepared together over the course of many weeks. I am terrified of being in front of people and having to speak. I've never been required to perform any such task as part of my academic studies.

This is the reward I get? It is much more like a punishment! I look down at my notes in my sweating hands. *I really wish Mom and I had been less wordy with my speech. The "short and sweet" approach would have been much better!*

For the first time that I can remember, I wish I had not excelled at something.

I look over at the teacher beside me. He is not just some guy who taught me science and math. He is one of those teachers who truly cares for his students. He has been such a big supporter of me in school. He also coached me on the basketball team, believing in my ability to play well and pursue academic projects above and beyond the usual coursework. He looks over at me and gives me a wink, as if to say, "It's going to be alright. You will do just fine."

My mind races, unable to hold onto that sentiment. I want his support to be comforting, but it is not! *I will be alright? Yeah, right!* I am sweating, dizzy, and nauseated. If I live through this without making a complete fool of myself, I will be surprised. My jacket is not helping the situation at all. *Teal is just not my color!* Black or gray would have been so much better and less noticeable. After I blunder through this failure of a speech, I'll be even easier for my classmates to find and mock after the ceremony. Others just assume I will do great at things. They believe in me.

Well, I have news for them.

As much as I try to hide the fact, my confidence fades with each passing moment. The impending doom of my speech begins to feel like freefalling from a skyscraper. It actually feels like my very life is in danger.

I will do anything to get out of this speech! But if I just run out of here, it will make everything worse! Everyone will see me. Everyone will be disappointed. Some may even be glad I messed up. *I will look like an idiot!*

So, I stay seated. I quietly hope one of two things will happen to prevent my inadequacy from being seen.

First, maybe it won't be so bad. Maybe I can get myself together enough to read my speech with minimal damage. Or, second, maybe the building will catch on fire, and we will all have to be evacuated. That is the more ideal solution. Of course, if the building does catch on fire, I'd like everyone to get out safely. God, you don't have to kill anyone over this. I am just spitballing some ideas for you to run with! It's a win-win situation! Come on! Help me out here! I just need a distraction so I won't pass out, puke, pee my pants, or forget how to read and speak.

I just want to escape this terrifying moment. I am desperate.

It's obvious nothing will actually happen to save me from my fate. Maybe it is for the best. Could this become a growth experience for me? Though I doubt public speaking will ever be a common occurrence for me, I could stand to learn from others more experienced than I. With that comforting thought in mind, I start observing the other speakers for pointers. Maybe I can learn something from them that will help me get through my own speech.

The lady from the County Board of Education is doing a fantastic job. I have no idea what her speech is about, as I am unable to focus on the actual words she is saying. But she looks and sounds great. The shoulder pads in her dress are a nice touch. It makes her look pretty tough, almost like a football player. *Why does that matter, you idiot? You aren't wearing shoulder pads!*

Before I know it, her speech is done and now the Salutatorian is stepping up for her turn. I know she's nervous only because she told me beforehand that she was. But now that she's up there, I cannot see it at all. If I could only pull that off, just like she is doing! The less that people notice how terrified I am, the better.

At this point, there is no way for me to hide all aspects of my fear and nervousness. It is all building up inside me like a bomb, ready to explode. I still need an approach that will save me. As the time for my own speech approaches, I think back to what my life-long best friend did earlier in the ceremony. He had the relatively easy task of introducing the lady from the Board of Education. I had previously dismissed his approach, believing it wouldn't suit my needs.

In short, Lavelle just got his speech done. No frills or bonuses. There were no glances up to the crowd in front of him. He had read straight from the paper he had it all written out on. In hindsight, it looked much like a hostage video. But I can't keep lying to myself that I can do any better. *Maybe I should just go with his approach.*

Truthfully, it was a genius strategy. Lavelle just got up there, read fast, and got out. At this point, I'm no longer concerned about doing a good job. *It is all about survival at this point. Lavelle knew it, and now I know it!*

It is time for awards to be presented. Due to my aptitude for academics, I receive several. At the end of each year, our teacher and principal issue out awards for each subject, one at a time. The principal would tell me not to leave the stage until I received several awards, thus saving me the trip of sitting down in between each one. I am used to this, and it has always been something of a running joke between me, my peers, and my teachers. Tonight is no different. I take my usual place, standing beside my teacher as he delivers several award certificates to me. The audience laughs and applauds at what is a culmination of my efforts over the course of the past 9 years.

This presentation of awards is very different for me. In the past, I wasn't bothered by the attention it generated. The awards helped remind me that I was significant in some way. Instead, tonight it only serves to remind me of my upcoming speech.

Why the heck did I do this to myself? These awards and recognition are surely not worth what I am going through tonight. I will gladly give this all up to escape having to make this speech.

Although this is meant to be an exciting and rewarding moment for me, I do not enjoy it at all. This night is intended to be a special culmination of my many years of hard work, but it is becoming something else to me entirely.

My final moments of reprieve come to an end as the presentation of awards is suddenly over. *My cue is coming up. When everyone sits down, I have to stand up and begin my speech!*

At this point, my memory becomes a complete blank for the space of several moments. I cannot recall standing up and approaching the podium, nor can I recall reading the opening sentences of my speech. I wouldn't be surprised if I began speaking before the audience had been fully seated after the awards. I do, however, remember the lines I keep repeating in my mind all throughout. *Remember my game plan. Get in, read fast, and get out.*

I can't read fast enough. My escape plan isn't working. After those first few sentences, I perceive a noticeable slowing of time. I can hear no other noise beyond the distant sound of my slurred voice, the unnaturally loud beating of my heart, and my labored breathing. I can't see it, but I know everyone in this auditorium is focused on me. In a moment of unconscious reflex, I break from my game plan and glance up for just a moment. I look out into the audience, curious to see what they think about me in this pinnacle moment of my entire academic career. If just one person smiles at me with even the remotest hint of encouragement, I may yet find the strength to get through this.

But that is not what I see. What I see is crippling. I see the look on everyone's faces that you expect when listening to a soloist singing completely out of tune in a choir at church. Most of the audience tries to feign indifference, but many are cringing and I feel like even a few are laughing quietly to one another.

Oh God, please do not let me pass out! I cannot move! I can barely breathe!

I read as fast as I can, which becomes more and more difficult as I blunder with increasing frequency. I lose my place several times. I misspeak words over and over, again. My trembling is totally apparent in my voice.

Why is this speech so long?

I stumble through the rest of the speech. Long before reaching the last line on the pages in front of me, I feel completely defeated. Everyone claps, but I can only imagine what they are actually thinking: Praise the Lord that uncomfortable part of the ceremony is finally over! Neil may be book smart, but that is about all he has got going for him.

And perhaps the worst of all: *I feel so sorry for him.*

❖ END TO PERFECTION ❖

That night, I felt humiliated. I owned that humiliation, which led to something for me that all of us have had a taste of at some point: a deep sense of shame. Adam and Eve experienced it for the first time after being deceived by Satan in the Garden of Eden, mistrusting God, and then partaking of the fruit that God had told them not to eat. While others may encounter it in a multitude of different ways, I experienced shame after a painful failure of a speech stripped me of the ability to continue hiding neatly behind a mask of being smart and obedient. From that event, the seed was planted deep inside me that there was something inherently wrong with me. I then believed I was not smart enough, I could not be successful, I was not acceptable just as I was, and in general, I was just not good enough. I carried that shame for many, many years. Numerous times something happened that caused me to think back and relive that speech, and all that came with it. Even thinking about it caused me to lower my head and cover my face.

Certainly, there had been dark moments in my life before that night. I call them dark because I stopped acknowledging that they had occurred. I had hidden those moments away so deep inside myself that I believed they could not hurt me anymore. However, those memories had implanted subtle-but-devastating lessons that I unknowingly carried into that botched speech, and I just could not find a way to bury that encounter on stage deep enough for it not to affect me. That experience in front of all those people served to amplify the inadequacies all of those other times could only whisper to me from the dark corners of my memory: *Neil, you are a complete failure. You are a pathetic and weak little boy. You are a fraud. You cannot do anything for yourself and never will. You are messed up and an overall bad person. Nothing will change that. You will never amount to anything. Everyone knows this, and finally you have realized it, too.*

Until that night I had excelled in almost everything I set my mind to for as long as I could remember. Sure, some of my peers had called me a nerd at times, but I could always brush that off. It was no big deal as long as I felt I could achieve respect in other ways. However, that night marked a change in my view of myself. Not only did I not excel at delivering a speech, I completely failed to prove how much I deserved those achievements in front of a large crowd of people. My failure made all of my accomplishments lose value. The identity I came to rely on lost its value in my eyes.

My perceived streak of perfection was over. I had failed, and failed miserably. I had discovered a great weakness, even though I did not have a name for it. Now, the only thing I could do was figure out how to deal with the resulting mess. How could I go forward and avoid such a catastrophe from happening again? I had no idea that incidents like the speech were only the beginning. Even after that night, experiences like that would continue to haunt me again and again. That pervasive and crippling fear would rob me of many times of joy and excitement in years to come. Those moments were only a sign of something much bigger that was buried deep inside of me.

THINGS TO THINK ABOUT

1) Can you think of a time in which you were frozen in fear? What happened?

_____
_____
_____

2) What personal failure in your life stands out as one that is hard to forget? Was it as a parent, child, employee, or some other role? What do you feel when you relive that memory?

_____
_____
_____

3) How was your experience similar to mine? How was it different for you?

_____
_____
_____

4) What did these experiences teach you about yourself at the time? Did you feel ashamed afterwards? What did you say to yourself? Did your self-image change?

_____
_____
_____

Open House

It is the Fall of 1992. Chris Farley has just been named as an official cast member on Saturday Night Live, Nirvana's song "Come As You Are" is a hit alternative rock song, George H. W. Bush is the president, and I've barely survived the first several weeks of my freshman year in high school. I am sitting in the classroom where my social studies class takes place. It happens to be Open House, a time in which parents come with their children to meet their teachers and discuss grades, behavior, and anything else that is pertinent to aid students in their high school experience.

I rub my head. It's something I do when I am nervous. I watch anxiously as my parents talk with my social studies teacher. I can't help but roll my eyes as I look at him. He's standing at the front of the room next to his podium, just as he does each day during class. The only unusual thing about him is he isn't wearing that ridiculous hat.

For some reason unbeknownst to us students, he often wears an engineer's cap to school. He is not an engineer, nor has he ever been. We checked.

I look down at my desktop, which is scratched badly at the top right-hand corner. It is obvious, at least to me, someone is trying to cover something with all those scratches. That "someone" is me. *Man, I hope that doesn't come up tonight in my parents' conversation with him...*

I am sitting with several of my classmates in the desks we carved our initials on only a few weeks ago. From one of them, I learned a lot of new things beyond how to carve initials into a desk with a knife. One of those things is cursing. He's great at it, and I acquired some of it for myself. Upon starting high school, I knew only a limited number of usable curse words. My offensive vocabulary is greatly expanded now thanks to him. I think it makes a real difference in helping me fit in.

We're all waiting for what I am now suffering through: our parents' update from the teacher we all ticked off when we decided to mess up his freshly-painted desktops. Just this past summer, he had taken the time to paint all of our desktops dark blue, our school color. When our teacher noticed initials in some of the desks, desperation inspired me to quickly scratch mine out so he would not realize I was one of the culprits. As far as I'm aware, he still doesn't know I am among those responsible.

But that isn't the worst of what I fear he'll tell my parents.

God, please don't let them find out how bad my grades are! I'll get them up, I promise. I will do better, and I won't vandalize any more desks either! Just get me out of this!

I pray my teacher will soften the blow somehow for Mom and Dad. At this point, I am almost certain this discussion will cease any hopes of ending my night on a good note. All I can hope for at this moment is to escape with minimal damage... something

I seem to do with increasing frequency of late. Operating on fear has a funny way of doing that to a person; instead of ever living and enjoying the moment, we constantly seek to escape it.

Maybe he will just tell them I am struggling with comprehending the material, and that is why my grades are so low. After all, he is still in the dark on the fact that I am guilty of carving my initials into one of his precious desktops.

I can't stand the fact that it is all out of my control at this point. When dealing with fear, we all want some sense of control. It makes us feel safer, even though in truth we aren't.

I whisper nervously with my classmates, people who I've been working hard to fit in with for several weeks. The carving of my initials wasn't my idea, but rather theirs, and they made fun of me for even hesitating to do it. I watch my parents' and my teacher's facial expressions at a distance, trying to interpret them and foresee just how much trouble I am in. My failed effort at analysis bugs me. I have found myself doing this a lot lately: trying to analyze anything that is a potential threat. I want to figure things out so I can be ahead of the game. However, the very act of doing this fuels my anxiety.

This is a whole new experience for me. In previous years, Open Houses proceeded very differently. I never had anything to worry about before. It was the same routine over and over: "He's such a great student. He behaves well, and his grades are excellent." Teachers took those opportunities to brag about me, my parents would beam with proud faces, and we would all go home happy.

Not this time. No, after this first Open House in high school, the conversation in the car on the way home will be much different. I can see the look of shock and anger on their faces. Since the beginning of this semester, I have lied repeatedly to them about how things are going at school, yet another behavioral pattern new to me and surprising to them. It's a necessary survival technique in my mind, intended to help me to avoid the consequences and hide the shame of the new approach I have with life.

After the failure of my 8th grade graduation speech, I strongly believed I needed to begin high school with a new attitude and identity. After that intense encounter with fear and failure, I sought to prepare myself mentally for high school. I'd done everything I could to put that embarrassing speech out of my mind, but with a major change of environment in front of me, it was difficult to do. Entering this new level of schooling stirred up yet another fear. Along with failure, I also feared the unknown. Many scary, disturbing thoughts ran through my head.

What's next? What is your next miserable failure? The last time, you did not even see it coming, you were not prepared, and look what happened! Now you are entering a new school, with new classes, with new classmates, with new teachers, and a whole bunch of other unknown stuff. You are not prepared! You will fail! You will not fit in, and you will look like an idiot!

I am terrified of change. When faced with the unfamiliarity of change, our minds run through endless possible scenarios that we can't help but worry about. Change introduces "unknown stuff," something that is very difficult, if not impossible, to prepare for. And after what I learned from my experience speaking to my graduating class, I really wanted to be prepared.

I turned to those around me for help before I began high school several weeks ago. The last time I did that, it had been on stage, when I silently took pointers from other speakers. I don't talk to anyone about my dependence on them and the examples they set for me. No one seems to even notice the anxiety I feel at times like that. People have no idea how dependent I am upon them. Even now, no one knows how terrified I am and how the changes I have made are nothing more than my best shot at dealing with all my fears.

With the impending doom of starting high school, I couldn't help but consider my best friend, Lavelle, for making my entry into a new school easier. At first, I thought that us both making the transition together would work perfectly, as he had been a reliable and exemplary friend for as long as I could remember. But this time, I couldn't look to him for help. We received our class schedules, and we had no classes together. Though I would frequently see him between classes, that wasn't enough to rely on him.

I've only had a few people I hold strong connections with. In the absence of Lavelle, I had few other options. Instead, I looked to my girlfriend to get me through the transition to the next stage in my life. 14 years is a young age to place one's own security upon members of the opposite sex. It didn't work, but, oh, did I try!

My thoughts at the time were, with her around I had something familiar going with me into this new phase in life. It calmed me down some. I could hang out with her between breaks and find the locations of classes when I got lost. Most importantly, with her around, I was not alone. She was like medicine for my anxiety.

And then it happened.

The one thing I wanted and needed to happen fell through, leaving me to face my fear alone. Our relationship, and my plan, blew up before I even had the chance to get started!

She broke up with me! Like an old Boyz II Men song, it led to an emotional time for me. It hurt. Her rejection made me feel like I'd lost everything. In my mind, I did lose everything. All of this happened mere days before my first day in high school! The discovery of my inadequacies that fateful night of graduation, coupled with the loss of the one I relied on to get me through this next big thing was too much. Again, my "smart, obedient" approach to life failed. Humiliation, failure, and now rejection!

That prompted the need for change, a major change. I needed a change big and bad enough to assure me safety from ever reliving how I felt that night at graduation. I needed a plan that would get me safely through this mountain in front of me. The last thing I wanted to do was feel the way I did during my speech and after my girlfriend broke up with me. I needed something to rely on, something to protect me and to numb me, if necessary, from the bad feelings that would come each day.

I was, and am, willing to do whatever it takes to avoid the things I am scared of. My high school career began with that promise. I want a definitive plan, but avoiding fear is very hard work! It morphs and surprises you along the way. It is impossible to be prepared all the time for all possible outcomes. Thus I have to settle for trial and error. I dodge my fears until I hit the sweet spot, when I find what works.

To avoid my fears, I have done several things. First, I vandalized a desktop to fit in with those I view as my peers and friends. Second, I incorporated as many curse words as I could into my dialogue to ditch the "well behaved" image. And third, I allowed my grades to plummet to avoid any sense of failure. Like with my speech, I feel that I will only look like a failure when I try. But if I don't try, no one, including me, will expect much.

At this moment, watching my parents and my teacher during Open House, I feel very much like I did before my speech. My mind is whirling. I am dizzy and sweating. I feel sick. *Maybe I can get out of this Open House without much being said. Maybe Mom and Dad will chalk it up to me needing more time to adjust.*

The last few weeks have been terrible, and now this! I think back to my first experiences with high school. I have been shoved into lockers by seniors. I have been bullied by a guy and his two "henchmen," just like it happens in the movies. I am scared to go to any after-school functions like dances and football games for fear of similar treatment. In trying to survive this daily battle and not be the nerd no one wants to be around, my grades are now terrible, and I have even driven my best friend away.

I cannot believe it, but I have even isolated myself from Lavelle, the most loyal friend I have ever known. It has not been on purpose, but with trying so hard to be someone different, I have failed to be a friend like I have been in the past. Needless to say, my plan is just not going well. And now I must face my parents' disappointment.

My parents have no idea what I have really been doing, because I have not told them. Not only do they not know about the bullying, they have no clue what my teachers will say of my academic habits. They only expect what they have seen in the past: exemplary grades and good behavior. But that is not at all what they will find.

As I strain, I can hear pieces of the conversation between my teacher and my parents. "He has a bad attitude and does not seem to care about the coursework," my teacher states simply. He then pointedly shows my grades to them in his little grade-book.

And with that, I immediately abandon any hope I held of salvaging the night. My teacher describes what he is seeing in my coursework and behavior. He does so bluntly, but accurately. He knows nothing of the "Valedictorian Neil", just like my parents know nothing of the new me. He has no clue that person ever existed. The shock on my parents' faces is evident throughout. They interrupt the conversation of grades to ensure he is talking about the right kid. Likewise, my teacher's expression turns to surprise as he notes the reaction. It is now evident to both parties that my behavior is both unusual and unexpected. I'm not sure how this will influence future interactions with my teacher, or the promised talking-to my parents no doubt plan to give me.

As reality sets in on the ride home, I watch as my parents endure the entire trip in silence, obviously deflated. The shame I now feel is so heavy I can barely sit up straight. I cannot breathe. I really want to cry, but I must not. If I allow myself to feel it, I am scared I will finally become overwhelmed with my lot in life. I cannot recall a time before this that I had so completely and thoroughly disappointed them. I, who had been the smart, obedient son, am now a disappointment! Not only that, I intentionally misled them for weeks to believe nothing was wrong!

The way I chose to respond to my fears is something I know will not be acceptable to my parents, nor should I expect it to be. I am deliberately putting off my responsibilities by not studying or putting forth an effort, being disrespectful to authority, and doing whatever else it takes in my mind to avoid rejection, failure, and humiliation.

❖ A NEW IDENTITY ❖

When you knowingly do wrong, you wind up with shame, and I had a lot of it. From that, I developed a way to avoid feeling it, to hide behind the mask of my new identity. Thus I established the pattern of lying. Each time I constructed a lie, I knew there would be a day when I was found out. I chose to put off dealing with that inevitable outcome. I engaged in total avoidance. "I don't care, I will deal with it later," I would say to myself. I painted the picture I knew others wanted to see, and sold it to them as best I could. I could not let my facade falter, for that had become my way of surviving daily.

I honestly cannot recall all that happened at home immediately after this dreadful event. I know my parents talked with me. I know they wanted answers. They so desperately wanted to understand what was going on. Yet, I felt so drenched in shame that I wanted to curl up into a ball and not speak to anyone for the rest of my life. Silence became my last refuge. I found over my teenage years, that it became one of my go-to approaches in enduring conversations in which I needed to avoid the fear and truth. Many times, it was all I had to survive. It helped me to avoid facing anything. With this dramatic episode of Open House behind me, I only perceived two possible choices. I knew I either had to drop this new approach to life and go back to my old grade school identity, or get better at this new one. But after how I felt during that speech, after being dumped, while trying to fit in and not quite being able to, and after constantly being called a dork and a nerd, I chose the latter.

I convinced myself the old identity just carried far too many let-downs. Even if all of that was the real me, I was willing to hide myself for the rest of my life if it meant being able to avoid the feelings of disappointment that came with it. I reasserted myself and recommitted to my vow to never be the "old Neil" again. Even after the humiliation of my parents' discovery of my failing grades, I would do everything in my power to avoid facing things of which I was scared. I would perfect this "new Neil", even if it was a complete masquerade.

I hoped my parents would change their view of me and accept me that way, like I was trying hard to do. Maybe one day they would just accept what I discovered about myself and drop the ridiculous notion that I had potential.

In my mind, my path was solidified. My perspective on life for many years was chosen. I was fully committed.

Terrified of failure and rejection, I no longer wanted to be the smart, obedient kid. Expectations on me were much too high that way. Failure was always imminent. This new identity had much less expectation. People would not expect so much, so I would not feel the pressure to excel. I could avoid humiliating experiences where people could see me fail, and I would be more accepted by my classmates for what I thought was a more natural identity.

I knew this outlook on life was going to be detrimental to my relationships and my future path into college and a career. But I chose to stuff all of that deep down inside of me. If I thought about it, I would not be able to push forward. I had to keep it together and lie my way out if necessary. I lied to others and to myself. Looking at the truth and the consequences of my actions would have required me to stop, and I did not want that. I could not do that.

I could not be humiliated again. I could not fail again.

Never again!

THINGS TO THINK ABOUT

1) When faced with fear, I developed a plan to avoid it. How did you learn to address fear? What is your approach to avoiding what you fear?

_____
_____
_____

2) I experienced much shame related to my fears and how I chose to avoid them. In my shame, I chose the avoidance tactic of lying. When have you experienced shame in your life? Was it because of something you did, or something done to you? How did you deal with this shame around others?

_____
_____
_____

(4)

The Back Row

"NEIL STUART MCLAMB."

I hear my name called from the podium at the front of the gymnasium. Anthony, a good friend of mine, marches slowly to my side in his suit. *Man, he is really dressed up.* I look down at my attire: khaki pants and a short-sleeved polo shirt, covered with a generous dose of Cool Water cologne. *I bet Mom is livid right now since I told her they said a suit was not necessary.*

When Anthony reaches me, he turns, I stand up, and we both ceremoniously march to the front. I rub my head nervously as he lights a candle and holds it out for me to take. *Great! Now, I have to hold this stupid thing the whole time without dropping it.*

The speaker continues to call names as Anthony marches me to the back row of the students already on stage recognized as new BETA Club inductees. This is relieving to me since I was hoping for such a location. My fears of being the center of attention are quite real, and being on the front row would only serve to bring back the still-fresh memories of my failed Valedictorian speech from two years ago. From this location, I can hide and escape the notice of my peers.

I look down at the candle in my hands. So much can go wrong with a simple candle! *I hope the wax does not drip on my shoes. What if I accidentally set the girl's hair in front of me on fire?* I hold the candle as still as possible, though my shaky hands, combined with the jumping flame still give me cause for concern.

The last of the names is called and the reigning BETA Club President begins his speech. I peek around at the audience, taking note of my parents. Mom wishes I had put on a suit. She doesn't understand. Looking as cool as possible is not easy. The key to my façade is not making it look like I'd tried really hard to get here. *Shoot, who cares how I look anyway? I don't!*

Unfortunately, the presentation of awards is not the only part of this event that I'm dreading. My unease is also largely due to the events that will take place after this ceremony, when the older members will go through the ritual of hazing. I've heard stories, and none of them are what I'd like to endure. It may be all fun and games for some, but not for me. Maybe I can blend in with the wall and they won't notice me. Anything to avoid them singling me out for the worst of the hazing! God, a little help, please?

Just get through the rest of this ceremony, let me live through the embarrassing crap afterwards, and I am done. God, hurry all this up so I can just go home.

Survive and advance, that's what I do in situations like this. There is no time to enjoy any of these so called "special experiences." I could not even imagine enjoying anything like this, really. It is like some sick plan to force me to be on guard, holding my breath until it is over. I am convinced there is only one way to handle times like this. My plan is the safest way. No risks. I do not want to look like an idiot again, and so far, my approach seems to have worked well.

However, as much as I want it to look like I don't care, I do still secretly hope my parents are proud of me, at least for putting in enough effort to be inducted into this honors society. Perhaps that can be some consolation for all the negative consequences that resulted from my quest for a new identity.

I've come a long way from the failing grades that I had those first few weeks of my freshman year. Based on the experience of my parents finding out about my failure, I had to make some modifications to how I approached this whole "high school experience." Now, I am being inducted into the BETA Club, all the while looking like I did not even try to get there. I consider this something of a triumph, the sweet spot that I am looking for.

THE "SWEET SPOT"

At this point, I had found what I considered the sweet spot. I did well enough to avoid disappointing and angering my parents further, while also being careful to avoid rejection for being a nerd or having to risk humiliation in front of my classmates again.

My grades weren't the only things I had to adjust in order to survive. Over the past two years since I began high school, my behavior had produced many challenges as well. Dealing with my fears had required a balancing of bad behavior and a good mask to hide them. I did not want my parents or anyone else who might disagree with my actions to see what was really going on. I wanted to sell everyone on the new identity that I was growing quite fond of. Unlike my old self, this one seemed to protect me from all the things I wanted to avoid: fear, disappointment, and rejection.

At this point, I was still working to perfect the guise, but it was coming along quite well. Although my external appearance created the illusion of a budding youth with potential, the reality of what was going on was much different. Since those first couple of months of high school, I continued to perfect the art of dishonesty.

I discovered a girl who wanted to be my girlfriend, and I had really latched onto her. Like my last girlfriend, she was my safety net, the person I fell back on to hide and recover from everything else. That was certainly not the role she deserved or was looking for. She took care of my strong need for acceptance when I could not find it anywhere else. She liked me, and that felt really good to a boy so desperate for validation of any kind. Her attention was so much better than the rejection I had experienced in the past, and having a girl who liked me made me feel sort of like a real man. That was something my failures told me I could never be.

I would do anything to maintain those good feelings. That included keeping the attention of a girl, holding true to my new image amongst my friends, and fooling whoever stood in my way. I lied more than I told the truth. I lied with my words, behavior, facial expressions, and just about anything I needed to in order to satisfy the person I was dealing with at the time. I lied because I desperately wanted to feel like they were on my side. I needed them to agree with me to validate what I was doing. The irresponsible, bad choices I made had to look okay or stay hidden completely not only to me, but to those who might disapprove.

I lied to my girlfriend when I treated her badly by flirting with other girls. Many times she would catch me, but I hid my disloyalty from her in an effort to assure myself that I would not lose her. Truthfully, it was so that I would not lose what I felt she had to offer me: the attention and all the good feelings that went with it. I selfishly craved all the attention I could get to make myself feel better. I was in no way a lady's man, but not for lack of trying. Although she was as committed as a teenager can be in a relationship, no girl could offer enough to satisfy my bottomless pit of neediness. So, I sought attention from any girl who would give me the time of day in an effort to feel whole.

I lied to my parents about my daily activities when I knew they would not approve. I even exaggerated to my friends about how my parents treated me. I vilified my parents, whenever possible, so that my peers felt sorry for me. When I could not participate in certain activities due to my parents, I shifted the blame to avoid looking like a loser. I discovered how a well-placed pity party could often manipulate others and get me what I wanted.

These lies were all based on fear, every single one of them. I did not take the time to consider the source of my dishonesty. Lying gave me a sense of control over the things I was troubled with. I was satisfied to some degree with my lifestyle. It worked! Why question it? That is the typical response of someone driven by fear. My priority was not to discover the root problem, but to treat the symptoms. At that time in my life, I chose to stay blind to my issues. I could not imagine an easier way to survive the rigors of adolescence than to get what I wanted while also avoiding what I did not want.

But if I had taken the time to understand myself, if something had jarred me enough, this is what I would have seen:

I was terrified of emotional rejection. Who doesn't fear this? We all seek to find our place, especially when we're experiencing such drastic changes during teenage years, both socially and physically. My solution was to protect myself from it. I latched onto the first girl who showed me attention. But eventually that was not enough. I felt constantly faced by the possibility that she could break up with me. To protect myself against that eventuality, I sought to secure acceptance from other girls as well, which resulted in mistreating and hurting my girlfriend and others repetitively. To maintain this behavior, I lied… a lot.

I also wanted to avoid being a failure. In trying to fit in, I worked hard to do "good enough" grade-wise to get some honors in school, but not too many so that people would make fun of me or call me a nerd. By accomplishing that plan, I discovered another part of my approach that I liked. It helped address my fear of failure. Knowing I was only giving partial effort, I could always tell myself I did not really fail. I simply said, "I could have done better if I had wanted to." I was even lying to myself! In many ways, I saw myself as a failure ever since that dark night during 8th grade graduation. Not only was that a total failure in my mind, it also brought to light other parts of me that were not good enough. So I hid behind my mask, on the back rows of life, so I did not have to face the fears that set me down this dark path. Again, understanding the source of my problems was not foremost in my mind. Why deal with them when I could just as easily keep them at a distance as long as I could?

Though I was terrified of looking like a nerd, I still also feared becoming a disappointment to my family. The result of my self-protection included many lies to keep my parents happy and my fear-avoiding lifestyle proceeding without interruption. I didn't escape notice completely, and unfortunately my parents learned pieces of the ugly truth many times throughout high school. The tales I spun to them were often made-up stories I devised simply to keep them happy. Of course, lies don't hold up forever. The cycle became one of my lying, my getting by with it a while, their finding out, my getting in trouble, and then my starting the lies again.

So what exactly was my approach to resolving my problem? It revolved around avoiding problems in the first place, effectively running away from situations in which I was faced with what I feared, or potentially could be faced with it. Looking back, it is easy to describe it in a few words, a mantra of sorts. Those words were, "I don't care."

I habitually said that motto to myself. I would sometimes even say it out aloud. I'd add explicit adjectives throughout to drive the point home even stronger, when necessary. I was constantly trying to convince myself, and others, that it was true. I needed to believe it to keep going. Without it, I feared becoming lost, left face-to-face with everything that I sought so hard to avoid.

Different people respond differently to fear. Some simply choose other ways to avoid fear. I have been told by some individuals that they chose to say they were sick and then left when faced with any fearful situation. Admittedly, this strategy didn't cross my mind back then. If it had, I think I might have used it some.

Some people have told me they took the complete opposite approach of how I approached my fears. When fear took over, rather than running from it or crumbling under the pressure, these individuals fought harder to overcome their circumstances and battle with the stress it created. Instead of avoiding failure with pacifism, they aggressively did things to avoid their fear from being realized. These individuals attempted to prove to themselves and others that they were not a failure. Rejection and failure weren't options, so they pushed to gain acceptance and success. It wasn't until later in life that I dabbled with this method.

Regardless of how we choose to respond when fear takes over, the end results are the same. Whether we passively or aggressively try to avoid it, "IT" is our focus. Though the consequences of the fears being in control may take years to manifest, they eventually do. The repercussions of a fear-focused life wear on us like a cancer. And since our approach to surviving these fears works for us in the present, we truck on like everything is okay, never expecting what lies ahead. No one around us does either.

Everyone chooses a different medicine for dealing with the pain of fear. In my case, I chose apathy. It was my sanctuary. It felt safe. And it was the socially-acceptable standpoint to hold during that part of the 90's, labeled the "grunge era" by some. Cool people were often identified by their "I don't care" attitude. I was able to use that to fit in as well. No longer the hard-working honors student, I became the "whatever, I don't care" guy who did well sometimes, but not because he was trying. If I did fail, it was because I didn't try, not because I was an inherent failure. It felt so right and so perfect!

I continued down this path for several more years. It led me into making decisions that I would not have made otherwise. Self-medicating with "I don't care" was not always enough. Sometimes that medication needed a little supplement to augment its effect. Though high school required little of it, if I was going to continue this way of dealing with my fears, my next step in life would demand it.

THINGS TO THINK ABOUT

1) I constantly went into "survival mode" seeking a way out of fearful situations. Do you remember times that, instead of being able to enjoy something, you found yourself merely "surviving it"? How did simply surviving feel as opposed to the thought of just facing your fears?

_____
_____

2) I found many ways to hide, avoiding fear and self-medicating my shame. I hid on back rows, behind lies, behind the acceptance of girls, and behind an "I don't care" mask. In what ways do you hide?

_____
_____
_____

(5)

Skipping Class

THE ALARM GOES OFF. I barely crack my eyes open. I reach over and hit the snooze button. *Oh man, I've only had…* I peer at the clock that reveals I have had only about three hours of sleep. I lay there and stare at the ceiling for a few minutes. *What should I do?* I roll over to my other side and crack the blinds, immediately blinded by the sun high above the horizon. The sunlight hurts my eyes. *Forget it. I just won't go to class*, I say to myself, for the millionth time. *Who cares?*

I end my half-hearted struggle with a question spawned from my "I don't care" approach. The answer to the question "Who cares?" is always "Not me!" I only set that alarm clock to make myself feel like I am actually trying. And, as crazy as it sounds, it seems to work.

I will get it together, just not today. Maybe tomorrow? Wait… ugh, not tomorrow. I have already missed that class so many times.

I could never convince that professor to allow me back in there. Why did I have to pick a university with an attendance policy?

I have missed so many classes, I've grown accustomed to begging and pleading with professors not to flunk me for excessive absences. The begging and pleading has included many pity parties and lies. So far, it has seemed to work. But I am reaching the end of my ability to deceive them. Thus far they have been kind, but they are smart. It won't take a genius to eventually catch on.

I do not feel like dealing with that. I will just wait until next week. I will get back on schedule and catch up all that I've missed.

I've gotten pretty good at lying to myself to silence any sense of responsibility and the shame that goes along with shunning it. When I started college a few months prior to this Fall morning in 1996, I faced a major change, and change is something I do not like! I had already learned that change brought with it many things I wanted to avoid! Change has all of these fears wrapped up in it, and more: the unknown, the renewed potential of failure, the probability of looking stupid, and the possibility of rejection. That is a lot to avoid!

I slowly sit up in my bed. I look around at the four block walls of my dorm room. *Oh, it feels good to be alone right now.*

My roommate had decided not to live in the dorm shortly before the semester began. So here I am, all by myself in my dorm room. I even have a bathroom to myself! How many college students can say they have that kind of living arrangement?

I don't mind being alone one bit. Truthfully I like being by myself. It makes it much more convenient to avoid things like social obligations. I have no one to ask me why I chose to avoid class again. I can literally hide out here until no one is in the halls to wonder where I have been and where I am going. I don't even need to make up any lies when I am alone, except the ones I tell myself.

What the heck happened last night? I ponder for a moment, then chuckle. *I can't remember!*

It feels good not being able to remember things. The short-term memory loss helps me to hide even more, ignoring responsibilities and feeling okay about it…at least for a while.

Last night I went out with some buddies of mine. I did not get back to the dorm until late…really late. Despite being an introvert, another reason why I enjoy being alone first thing in the morning, I have begun to really depend on my time with a few people to help me forget what I am doing (or not doing). They have no idea, and I have no intention of telling them. If they knew, they would point out how stupid I am acting, and I don't want that added baggage! I only want to hear what I want to hear.

Without consciously thinking about or acknowledging any of that stuff, I have been skipping classes since my first week in college. I use my catch phrase so often I've convinced myself I do not care about anything. More than anything I value the avoidance of being in a situation in which I have to face my fears. I am willing to do just about anything to keep myself safe from those things I fear most.

The first part of my college years has become much like the first semester of high school. This time, however, the hole I have dug for myself is so deep, it will take much more of an effort to get out. In high school, I could turn it around fairly quickly, but this is college… a whole different scenario.

Although the "I don't care" attitude seemed to work perfectly for me in the past, now it doesn't do enough to numb the feelings that creep up sometimes. Some mornings I wake and think, *Holy crap! What have I done?* I panic in these moments, but only for a short time. To avoid those surges of anxiety when reality threatens to reveal itself, I need something to supplement my "I don't care" approach. I have begun to rely on a specific snooze for my body's natural "alarm clock," to further delay having to wake up and deal with anything.

I continue to sit on my dorm room bed, still not wanting to get going. I ponder, *If not class, what will I do today?*

I sit here thinking about my day ahead, acting like I have something more important to do than attend class. Fooling myself, really. I already know the answer to my question. I intend to do the same thing I did the day before. I start out with "not caring about anything," and I stay the course. I will start my day by getting something to munch on for breakfast and proceed throughout the day while avoiding anything that might remind me of what I should be doing.

Man, I hope I can get up with some of the guys. Hey, but if it doesn't work out, I do have just a little bit of weed left!

I love zoning out with marijuana. I tried it a couple of times during my senior year of high school. At first, I did it out of curiosity, and because I saw it as an opportunity to get some acceptance from my peers. It is the 90's, and weed is considered "cool." However, in my first few weeks of college, it has become more than just an occasional way to fit in for me. It is medication for whatever ails me. And what usually ails me is fear.

Now, numbing myself with alcohol and drugs is a common occurrence...more so than I'd like to admit. I self-medicate almost on a daily basis, to some extent. Some days it is a few hits or drinks. Other days I get wiped out completely.

All people, when driven by fear, don't typically turn to irresponsibility, alcohol, and drugs, as much as I do. There are other ways to numb one's self. Many of these are much more socially-acceptable behaviors. Work, sex, pornography, video games, cleaning the house, taking risks, excessive exercising, and under- or over-eating are just a few of the options available. Basically, just about anything, good or bad, can be used to self-medicate when faced with fear.

This morning appears to be no different from any other morning during my first semester of college. However, on this particular morning, the small University I attend is holding a "Parents' Day," in which Mom and Dad are invited to attend the school and meet my instructors and other staff. Unsurprisingly, with the way I regularly missed class, my grades are low... really low. They are even worse than when I first began developing my "I don't care" attitude in high school.

And once again, my parents have no idea what is really going on with me at school. None. As attentive and involved as they have been throughout my life, I continue to hide many things from them, including the complete abandonment of all responsibility regarding coursework this first semester.

❖ PRESSING SNOOZE ❖

What happened next was eerily reminiscent of my "Open House" experience in high school. It was as if the cycle of rebellion was repeating itself. Looking back on it, it was! Of course, my parents were shocked, once again. That experience completely threw them for a loop. They knew I was combating certain struggles, but they had no idea I was skipping and failing classes. I put so much energy into lying and hiding things from them, that there was no way for them to conceive what was really going on until faced with the reality directly from my instructors. But until those fateful moments, whatever I thought they wanted to hear, I told them.

How could I not see this coming? Well, deep down, I did. I always knew a day of reckoning was coming with each lie I made up. Bad choices equate with comparably-bad consequences. I experienced it many times. But I avoided thoughts of that as well. I could have seen it, but I chose not to. I did everything I could to avoid looking at it. That was something I chose to be blind to at the time, as much as humanly possible. I had found a way to do it: "I don't care!" However, as much as I did not want to care, I did. I just refused to face the challenge of facing that fact amidst the predicament I had gotten myself into. I felt that I was too far in it to turn back!

I became so focused on my fears and running away from them that I dedicated myself to hitting any snooze button, including substance abuse, lies, and other avoidance behavior, that would delay my having to deal with any of it. I refused to see the blatant truth that was right in front of me. If I would have only looked a few steps ahead, I could have seen this path was not taking me to a good place. However, I did not want to look ahead. I did not want to believe for a second that my actions would hold a long-term adverse effect! I wanted to feel okay immediately, in the moment, and that meant not looking at anything that deterred me from that goal.

Much of that time period in my life is a blur. With the need to avoid reality in any way possible, I succeeded in leaving few things to memory. In talking with my wife, who was my then-girlfriend, my parents, and a few others who were close to me, I learned what others saw in me back then. It amazes me to hear from others just how well-hidden I was from the ones who loved me most. Although there were plenty of occasions when family became suspicious, no one knew exactly what was going on with me. In truth, I did not even truly know myself. When you hide from others, you must hide from yourself as well.

Of course, my parents went through many more disturbing realizations, dealing with the mounting stresses. Even in those moments where they questioned what was going on, I quickly came up with something to hide myself again and satisfy their concerns.

My girlfriend had a bit more insight into what was happening, but not much. I lied and hid things from her. This was a young lady who knew me in high school, as well as anyone could at the time. Now, she saw more and more of someone she did not know. She was looking at a mask, a mask I was developing as I went. She knew I was covering up something.

Lavelle, my best friend, a guy who had stuck with me through thick and thin throughout my life, did not see much of me during that time. When he did, all he saw was a guy with a "care-free attitude." But it was more than that, and he knew it. He knew me too well for me to completely hide that something was wrong. But I ignored the fact that something was wrong. I just told everyone and myself everything was okay.

Even after Parents' Day, for many months I continued with my advanced approach to "not caring." I didn't rebound as well as I did after Open House in high school. Back then, I was able to revise my approach to a point that it worked to postpone having to experience the frequently-surfacing consequences. This time around, I succeeded only in thoroughly numbing myself to anything and everything that caused me feelings of failure or rejection. I no longer felt the weight of shame that should have been there to remind me of the choices I was making. "I don't care" was both my mantra and my mindset. I hid behind anything I could. I refused to face anything that was even remotely a challenge.

I would not risk being found out. Occasionally my mask would slip enough for others to see a glimpse of what I hid deep inside, and those moments were horrendous. That was the one thing I could not seem to rid myself of: the consequences of my actions always caught up to me eventually. I could put them off, but they would rear their ugly heads, and it hurt when they did. It hurt really badly. The things I wanted to avoid, the very things I ran from, would violently slap me in the face when my charade would fail me.

Invariably, I lost the scholarship the university had so kindly awarded to me upon entry. Truthfully, I should have been kicked out of school for my irresponsible behavior. But due to the beneficence of professors, other staff, and my parents, it was decided to give me more chances than my actions deserved. My relationships with everyone I knew suffered greatly. They no longer knew me for who I really was, even when they thought they did.

It is impossible to have a deep, meaningful relationship with a person always hiding behind a mask. You can admire the mask, but you never get a chance to see the face behind it. In my case, the mask was thick. No one saw the real Neil.

THINGS TO THINK ABOUT

1) I got to a point that my previous ways of avoiding fears did not work. I began numbing myself further with things like drugs, alcohol, and more irresponsible behavior. However, there are many other forms of "self medication" other than drugs. When nothing else seems to calm your fears, what do you do? How do you "self medicate"?

_____

_____

2) Although my facade broke down at times, I hid so well that most people had no idea what was going on. I even lied to myself in order to avoid facing reality. What do you tell yourself and others when you want to hide your feelings of inadequacy or shame? How do you "press snooze" in order to avoid reality for just a little while longer?

_____

_____

_____

(6)

Building Rome in a Day

*W*HAT THE HECK IS THIS? I think to myself as I look over the exam in front of me. *Why did I even bother studying? I spent all of the last few nights committing course material to memory and none of the details I studied are even on here!*

I look up at the professor who sits at the front of the theater-styled classroom. She lounges up there, smug as can be. *I hope she's happy! All this hard work I have been putting into making all A's in Grad School, and it is all going down the drain because she wanted to prove some point to me and my classmates! What point is she even trying to make? I will just tell her what I think of her. No, I cannot do that. It will ruin any chance I have of pulling this grade up! I'm pretty much screwed!*

Over the last two years, things have changed drastically. I have gone from barely making it through the first two years of college to doing extremely well. At this point, my performance in grad school is the exact opposite of what I did before. In fact, I have all A's. It feels like so many years have passed since I was a "good student."

As I sit here staring at a test I am certain I cannot pass, I cannot shake the overwhelming feelings of anger that rage within my mind. This test will get in the way of my perfect finish to college.

Just my luck! No matter what I do, I lose. If I don't screw it up, something or someone else steps in and makes sure it gets screwed up for me!

Why God, why? Why do You do this to me? Am I not doing better? Is this not enough for You? I have worked my butt off the past couple of years! I have gotten my life straightened out, and this is the result I get? Are you still not pleased with me?! Can You not at least reward my hard work with not allowing this bitter professor to do this to me? She is the enemy here. Please do not let her win. Please fix this for me now. You can still give me a good grade if you want to. Come on... please God! Get me through this! You know I cannot handle what will happen if I fail this dang test!

That isn't the nice, polite, and reverent prayer I am taught to do in church. It isn't the nice little "wrap-up the day prayer" I occasionally say to Him at night, on those rare moments when I remember to do it. But it is proof of the direction the conversations I have had with Him have gone in recent years. I have told Him so many times that I did not care and I thought He didn't either. After a semester or two of working hard and seeing I can still produce good grades, I began to think maybe He did truly care. But this test sends me the message that He is still bent on tripping me up. It occurs to me that this may be the final moment of failure to prove that my best effort is not enough.

This isn't the first time I have cried out to or even at Him. I do this when I am in desperate need of help, like when I have to give a speech, when I am facing getting caught for doing something wrong, or when I am having one of those difficult times in the restroom. You know what I'm talking about. *God, I will never do this again if You will get me through this!* My talks with Him are primarily consistent of pleas rather than thanksgiving. He seems so distant and cold, the best I can hope for is to beg for Him not to smack me around or let me get hurt. I promise Him better behavior in exchange for these things, as if my relationship with Him is some kind of bartering agreement. I truly believe, with everything in me, that's what he wants.

I can't pass this test. I should have studied more, a lot more. Maybe I should just give up and walk out. As I look back down at this ridiculous exam, my old "I don't care" method of dealing with things feels a bit enticing for the first time in a while. I really just want to escape and not think about it anymore. The thoughts of failure are overwhelming.

But I can't just give up. I have come too far to give up now. I am finally close to proving that I am not a complete failure. I do not want to feel like I did a few years ago when I realized how much of an idiot I had become. I have to finish this thing. I try skipping throughout the test to find answers I know, to build some momentum and get my mind working. However, I find no such part, forcing me back to the beginning where I can only make the best guesses my mind can rationalize. I push through this thing, one question at a time. As I do, I keep hoping I will hit a question that I actually feel confident about.

All I can hope for at this point is a major grading curve. I can't doubt that this hateful professor will give us a curve. Or maybe, just maybe, I will have some actual luck and make good guesses, and do well enough I can bring my final grade up with other assignments. I look around at my classmates. I see them sweating as well. At least I will not be alone in failing this thing. There are people in this course who've sat for the Bar Exam! Even they are having a tough time, and they're lawyers!

❖ DRIVEN TO PERFORM ❖

Since my first few semesters of college, events had prompted me to change from my "I don't care" attitude. Simply put, the strategy finally reached a point where it no longer produced the result I so desired. I could no longer shake the anxiety that came with knowing I was being irresponsible and lying to everyone. As much as the indifference, drugs, and alcohol seemed to repress my self-loathing, they gradually ceased to produce that effect. In fact, I began having more issues, even when I got high.

The friends I hung out with were disappearing from my life, so I couldn't rely on them to escape. When I sought an escape with a joint or a drink, I began to have weird episodes that freaked me out. I would get dizzy, feel sick, and become disoriented as if in preparation for passing out. I eventually realized that instead of relieving my anxiety like it used to, the substance abuse made it worse, causing the new physical symptoms.

I reached a point in which I had to change, or I would not have been able to retain my sanity or end college with the degree or experience needed to get a decent job.

Toward the end of my freshman year, I finally got up the nerve to marry the wonderful lady who saw more in me than I saw in myself. We had our only son soon afterward. This forced a new perspective to my life that I was having a difficult time embracing. My "I don't care" attitude really doesn't fit with being a husband and father. I could not make indifference look cool and acceptable anymore, especially to myself. Although this was a difficult time for us since we were young, still in school, and busy with work, my wife and I were happy together. We had no clue what we had gotten into at such a young age, with everything that was going on. And yet, despite any hardships that came from our living conditions and youthful ignorance, her love and patience with me endured through the years and still astounds me.

My perspective on surviving had reached its limits and needed revising in a major way. It was time for me to clean up. I went through the very difficult and painful period of time when I quit using any drugs and alcohol, cold-turkey. I do not advise that strategy to anyone. Some professional help would have been very wise to help me get to the bottom of why I used them, but I was not done with hiding just yet. Getting help would have meant telling others what I had been doing.

Throughout the months of learning to live without that crutch, I also pushed myself to start trying harder in school. I saw glimmers of hope that I still had it in me to finish better than I started, so I pushed forward more and more. I was granted a good internship at a business in town. I retook several classes in order to bring my cumulative GPA up, and I made the major decision to enter grad school upon approaching the end of my four-year degree. Everything about me seemed revitalized. I believed I was finally on the right track.

If I could no longer avoid failure by running from responsibilities, I would avoid it by working so darn hard that failure became highly unlikely. The stress of this approach was not something I anticipated. I thought the success I would incur would be enough to take care of that.

Although I still strived to maintain an outer appearance that was easy-going and care-free, inside I was a basket case bent on performing to the best of my ability. Where "not trying" had been my focus before… "trying really hard" became my obsession. Of course, I did not acknowledge this to others, or even myself. Nothing less than the very best was acceptable to me. Although I thought it was helpful and motivational, the comments I would say to myself were more like a whip to keep me going. I constantly badgered myself with statements full of guilt and shame like "my family deserves only the best" and "I've got a lot to do to make up for my past".

The test I was so angry about led to a "C" in the course. There was a pathetically-small grading curve that really did not help much. The professor was intent on making a point. I am sure it was a good one. Too bad no one in the class understood the point. I was not happy. But with my new driven approach, I couldn't let that sway my momentum, and I kept pushing forward. I could see the light at the end of the tunnel, and I was not going to stop.

I did not realize it, but I was still just trying to survive. That had not changed. It's impossible to enjoy anything when you are constantly holding your breath, gritting your teeth with the gas pedal to the floor, just hoping to "get by" without crashing and burning. That is a stressful way to live. I had no idea all of this I was storing up inside of me would explode a few years later. There is only so much anyone can hide away inside.

Graduation came and went. My family threw a party to celebrate this monumental achievement in what had many times felt like an uncertain possibility. I don't care much for being the center of attention, but it was nice to have that recognition as "not a failure." That is how I saw it, anyway. Everyone who loved me was proud of me, but I was simply thinking, I'm not a complete loser...yay, with a hint of sarcasm. My fears had not really changed at all, even though my approach to them was different. That "C" turned out to be the only grade I got that was not an "A" in all of my grad school classes. I felt no moral problem writing that off as the professor's fault. Blaming her was important to me since any sub-par performance was considered evidence that I was inadequate.

The next step in life was finding a job. I had settled on a certain major in school and would pursue a career comparable to my education. I floundered a bit during the initial job search, but I was finally given a job through a man who had given me an internship a few years before. Everything should have been smooth sailing. Instead, after a few years, my next challenge was to be the startling realization that life as I knew it was coming to a close. Everything was not as okay as it seemed, and that was finally about to become very apparent.

THINGS TO THINK ABOUT

1) I had a new approach, but my fears and shame did not go away. I had just changed my way of dealing with them. Although I strived to maintain my "laid-back mask" for others to see, on the inside I was very driven to perform at a high level. Many people do this rather than succumbing to be irresponsible. Is this something you see in yourself? Can you remember a time in which you were driven to avoid failure and/or rejection by working hard to attain success and/or acceptance?

_____

_____

2) Anger was a sign that I still had a problem. This was apparent when the test I was taking threatened to mess up my "plan." Take a look at times in which you became very angry. Did someone or something block your goal to succeed or be accepted?

_____

_____

3) Do you ever get angry with God when you feel you have worked hard to improve your behavior but you still do not get what you want? Do you see yourself feeling like God is only pleased with you if your circumstances in life are good?

_____

_____

4) Although it was not as apparent as before, my fears were alive and well even in perceived successes. They still controlled my decision-making. What big decisions have you made in life based on fear?

_____

_____

(7)

The Snowball Effect

I AWAKE TO A FORCE THAT IS NOT IMMEDIATELY APPARENT. I CAN'T BREATHE. I struggle with each breath, but it just isn't enough. I feel like I'm suffocating, as if some tremendous pressure is on my chest and I am convinced no amount of air is enough. *Oh, God, not again.* I now know this feeling all too well. I look over at the red digits on my alarm clock. 12:05.

I surge out of bed and stagger to my feet before I make my way to the bathroom. I am dizzy and disoriented to the point where I almost hit my head on the doorway. I shake my head quickly a few times, trying to snap out of it. *Not again. Jesus, please, give me a break!*

I repeat the same phrase over and over. *God, please help me. Lord, God, help me.* I splash cold water on my face and look in the mirror at the pale face looking back at me. Something looks… not quite right. *Is that really me?* I barely recognize myself. This is all like a bad dream. But I know it's not. This is all too real, and it's not the first time I have gone through this.

My mind is awash in a sea of madness. The thoughts going through my head are weird. Most of them make no sense: quick flashes of images, song lyrics, and other things I can't make sense of. Everything is moving so fast that I cannot stop to ponder any of them.

I attempt to focus on one thing, to simply make it all stop. Then an annoying song gets stuck in my head, the same lyric repeating over and over. *Shut up!*

I place two fingers over my left wrist and check my pulse. Whatever is happening, I've achieved a record speed for heart rate. *Holy crap, I am going to die this time.* Now my heart is beating so hard that I don't have to check for a pulse any longer. I can feel it pounding on my chest, as if with every beat it is getting closer and closer to exploding.

I am suddenly light-headed as my heart skips a beat. *Oh no! What the heck was that?* I refocus my efforts from simply staying upright to instead avoiding another skipped beat, as if through the power of my mind I can control it. Each time it feels like my heart may skip a beat again, I cough loudly, as if that is enough to prevent it.

I turn to look at my wife, asleep—totally unaware of my struggle. She loves me so much, but how long can she really keep putting up with me? Something is incredibly wrong with her husband. He is dying, crazy, or possessed. There is no good explanation for these... "episodes."

I can't let her see me like this. I don't want her to wake up and watch me engage in these odd activities I do to survive through such an event. I definitely do not want her to wake up to watch me die! I quickly hurry into the den.

God protect me. Please! I know you can do it. I believe you can do it! Is this a demon attacking me? Is that what it is? God, please don't let me see it! If I see it, I don't think I'll have the fortitude to fend off my fear any longer! I glance around, checking every shadow to ensure it's not a manifestation of something from the spirit world sent to torture and possibly kill me.

I am completely in a frantic state at this point. I shudder uncontrollably, as if I am freezing. But I'm not. Well, maybe I am... I don't know! One minute I'm cold, the next I am burning up.

Now I am extremely angry. I want to punch something, or someone. *I need my sleep! But no, here I am awake and freaking out every flipping night of my life. Thanks a lot God for the help.* I clench both of my fists and hunch down like I am ready to slam into the offensive line of an opposing football team.

I immediately feel bad for such untoward thoughts about God. I am also very scared of Him being angry. What if He allows something bad happen to me? What if, in response to my irreverent words and behavior, He gives up on me? What if He kills me like He did Lot's wife in the Bible? *God forgive me, I am sorry! I am just frustrated about all of this. I don't know what to do!*

❖LIVING IN A FOG❖

That was me, late into 2003. I came to expect these odd events on a semi-regular basis. They were becoming more and more common. Shortly after falling asleep at night, I would wake up in a panic. I had no idea what was going on. It scared me beyond anything I had ever experienced. Public speaking seemed like a breeze compared to thinking I was going to die every night when I fell asleep.

The worst part of these attacks would last anywhere from fifteen minutes to an hour. But even after the hardest point, at times they would keep me up all night. The following days after an attack were like a blur. With very little sleep, I was like a zombie. I was exhausted all the time. Something called "brain fog" kept me from enjoying anything. Basically, it is a combination of bizarre sensations in your head that make it difficult to think clearly. It is like trying to experience each day, from simple conversations to work, with a mind full of hazy and confusing thoughts.

The attacks took something out of me that no amount of rest could fill back up. I needed an uninterrupted night of sleep, and those had become a carrot dangling just out of reach.

I refused to consider medical treatment, for fear of the diagnosis. I knew something was wrong with me, but I didn't want to know how bad it actually was. Either they would find out I had a terminal illness or they would find nothing. No amount of surgery would be able to fix what I felt. If what I had did not prove to be fatal, it meant I was mentally unstable, haunted by demons, or God was punishing me for something.

I was convinced God was ultimately responsible for these episodes. Either He was orchestrating them Himself, out of his anger and disgust with me, or He was allowing it because He did not see any good reason to intervene. Maybe He was waiting on me to somehow mend my relationship with Him. I simply had not done enough yet to feel like I deserved His help. I thought I deserved everything that was happening to me and that would be my life from then on. I had no clue what "just getting by" meant until then. I redefined "survival mode" in an effort to deal with the ever-increasing moments of terror.

There didn't seem to be a rhyme or reason to these episodes. My wife and I were puzzled by them. They only occurred at night for a while. Sometimes they occurred after a seemingly good day, others after bad ones. I simply couldn't identify any obvious contributing factors leading up to these moments.

When 2004 rolled around, I had my first daytime experience with one of them. That changed everything. At night at home, I was able to hide anything that happened. But when it became apparent they could occur anytime, anywhere, I was petrified. Others were going to find out that there really was something wrong with me.

The opening chapter of this book described my first daytime attack. It occurred one evening when my wife and I had gone out with our friends, Lavelle and Kelly. They were among the first to know my secret. At that particular point in my life, I had graduated from college only two years earlier. I had an office job in town, not far from our home. I thought things were going well. Melissa and I were well on our way to building a new home together. We were excited about moving out of our little trailer into something more spacious.

I felt fearful of many things in the past, like failure and rejection. I knew what it felt like to be scared, but I always found a way to avoid my fears. Suddenly, just as things in life seemed to be coming together, I was stopped cold by these paralyzing attacks that I could not explain. I couldn't avoid them because the cause wasn't apparent to me. How can you fix what you can't find? There was no way to self-medicate that would make me feel better.

I couldn't consider illicit drugs. I had tossed that idea out long ago as it was of no use to me anymore. Using drugs in college had just been a bad decision on my part, and the consequences were not worth it. I knew that stuff would no longer work for me anyway, given my current lifestyle.

The "I don't care" approach had also been put away long ago, but I could have pulled it back out. But what good would that have done against the overpowering, out-of-control attacks I was suffering through? I could have said, "I don't care" one hundred times in the middle of an attack, and it would have yielded the same result as firing a Nerf gun at a brick wall. Nope, that was not helpful at all.

I was backed into a corner. I could not avoid these surprise attacks. And having no plan to deal with these events scared me even more. I needed to figure out what caused them.

This fear of pending attacks gradually left me in a constant state of anxiety. I always wondered when my next attack would hit. It was like a snowball rolling down a hill. The fear got bigger and bigger as time passed, except there was no end to the hill. Every day that passed uneventfully was one day closer to what would be the scariest day of my life. I saw no end to my torment.

What I didn't know at the time was that all of this had been building up for a very, very long time. Just as life seemed to be reaching a point in which I could sit back and relax some, what I had been holding back for years was finally let loose. My strategies of avoiding everything I feared had reached a tipping point and my mind and body could no longer stand it. I had unknowingly allowed my fears to grow to enormous levels with the snowball effect. I had become a time bomb ready to explode, and I was in the final seconds. And explode, it did… in the form of panic attacks. I could not see the true cause of my panic because I had buried it deep. It would be another year before any of the real reasons would be revealed.

I spent a lot of time reflecting in self-contemplation. I sorted through a vast array of causes and effects of my life decisions. Early on, I believed my temporary stint of drug use had really messed me up somehow. Whether mentally or physically, they could have done some serious damage. Yet the question always came to me, "Why did that not show up before now?" I had stopped using drugs years before my first panic attack.

Then I considered the stress in my life. Many people remarked about how stressful my life must be. I got married and had a child at a very young age. My wife and I worked hard to finish college, and then we put a lot of effort into our full-time jobs. I thought, at times, that maybe those people were right. Perhaps I was just stressed from those things. But I saw other people in more stressful situations, and they were not running around like maniacs, hiding from everyone, and looking about for demons!

I suspected these attacks were something else, but I had no idea what. That's when the next chapter in my life began, when I started a rigorous search for an answer. I knew there was a reason for my current affliction, and when I found the cause, I also knew there would be a cure. I was determined to find it!

THINGS TO THINK ABOUT

1) I unknowingly allowed my fears to grow into gigantic monsters. The further we run from our fears, the bigger they become. When you look back on your life, what fears do you see yourself running from? What might you be running from now? Have you noticed your fears have grown scarier the more you have tried to avoid them?

_____

_____

2) Eventually, my pent-up fears exploded into panic attacks and almost-constant daily anxiety. Others experience this snowball effect in other ways, such as outbursts of anger, crying spells, cutting, eating too much, not eating enough, isolation from others/running away, behavior that resembles obsessive-compulsive tendencies (everything has to be in "it's place"). How does your mind and body respond to an overload of stress?

_____

_____

(8)

The Search

I TYPE THE WORDS "DIZZINESS AND BRAIN FOG" INTO THE SEARCH ENGINE ON MY COMPUTER AND CLICK "ENTER." In my extensive research online, I have identified these symptoms as two of the most troublesome with which I struggle. At this point, I feel that if I could rid myself of just these two things, my life would be considerably more bearable. I scan the results of the search on the screen. There are thousands of pages. I decide to click on one of the links near the top.

The heading of the webpage reads, "Candida overgrowth in the intestines." I scan the summary. Apparently this is something many people struggle with, many without realizing it. It is some type of condition where a person has an overgrowth of yeast known as candida in their intestines, resulting in all sorts of problems.

With it is a list of symptoms beyond dizziness and brain fog. *Hmmm…digestive problems. I do have a lot of digestive issues! My stomach hurts all the time! It is often upset! Shoot, it's rumbling right now!* I get moderately excited, as this may finally be the answer I am looking for.

It also causes 'irritability, depression, mood swings, and anxiety'… I have all of those. 'Difficulty concentrating'… check! 'Lack of focus'… yep, got that one too. I am even more excited as these symptoms match up perfectly with what I am experiencing.

Wait… *skin rashes?* For a moment, my heart sinks. I am disappointed. *Uhhh, do I have those? Yeah, definitely! Sometimes when I get out of a hot shower, my skin has those red blotches on it!* I quickly revert back to being almost convinced this is a plausible explanation for all of the ailments I've struggled with for many months.

'Skin and nail fungus infections.' Crap! That one does not fit at all. But, it does say right there that these are only possible symptoms. That means I don't have to have them all to diagnose myself with Candida problems. Still I have so many of the symptoms listed that this has to be what I am looking for! The realization that I only need some of these symptoms to have this disorder seals the deal. *I have Candida overgrowth! That's why I have these weird attacks and feel crappy all the time!*

I begin scanning for the treatment section of the website. I am following the well-developed method of self-diagnosis that I have grown accustom to using. I come up with a list of all the symptoms I have, research a possible cause, and then look up how to treat it.

A list of natural remedies are associated with this particular disorder. I begin writing them down. Just to make sure, I visit several other websites about this illness that suggest a special diet. I take down more notes. Treatments basically entail avoiding certain foods and eating more of another. *No problem, anything to feel better!*

Thank God, I can purchase all of the needed supplements online, so I don't have to go anywhere to get them. My anxiety is so bad right now that I cannot imagine having to walk the aisles of a store and search for anything. Sure, I've spent countless dollars on supplements for various possible ailments that I have self-diagnosed, but it all will be worth it when I finally find the right treatment!

Once I get all of this stuff in the mail and take these remedies, I'll finally be healed! As I look at everything in my browser shopping cart, I decide to just order and take them all. *Why waste time trying one at a time?* If for some reason this doesn't work, I'd rather know sooner than later, because I have a long list of possible illnesses to treat.

God, please let this be it! Let this be the end of this nightmare! I make sure to keep God in the loop on this. I am scared not to for fear of Him sabotaging me as a form of punishment. I have got to try to keep Him happy to increase the chances of getting out of this hell I am in. It's really no different than how I have strived to keep Him pleased so that I do not wind up in the literal hell one day. It is a stressful way to live, but what else can I do? I picture Him in a cloud, waiting for me to do something good or bad. When I do something good, I see Him barely nodding His head as if to say, "Finally, what took you so long?" When I do something bad, I see Him with a lightning bolt in His hand!

The last thing I need now is for Him to be upset with me about something. God helps those who help themselves, right? That's not specifically in the Bible, but it makes sense! That's why I stay "all prayed up" and working hard to find a solution. If I do the right things and stay on top of the search for a solution, I know God will fix this for me. It's all mysterious and difficult to maneuver because I don't know all the hoops I think He wants me to jump through, but I am trying. But the only other alternative would be to revert back to how things were before, when I neglected to please Him and possibly contributed further to my grief for not putting forth the effort to do so.

❖ MAZE OF MEDICINE ❖

At that point in time, I was only a few months into a frantic search for a cure. After cycling through other self-medicating approaches like the "I don't care" and "building Rome in a day" mentalities, it became my obsession to search for a medical condition to explain my problems and find some supplement to treat it. Prior to the panic attacks hitting, I self-medicated primarily to address the fear and anxiety I felt on an almost constant basis.

The panic attacks not only persisted, they increased in number. I had them every day, many times more than one, both day and night. Even when I wasn't having a full-blown attack, my general anxiety levels were debilitating. I could not imagine being able to do things that were once so simple, such as going to the grocery store, talking on the phone, going out to eat with my family, hanging out with friends, sitting in church throughout an entire service, or even walking to the mailbox on some days.

I was terrified of having an attack, or even publicly showing some of the other anxiety symptoms I found particularly embarrassing and bizarre. I was so dizzy and disoriented at times, that I could not generate a coherent thought, let alone hold a dialogue with someone. My voice would become shaky and I developed a nervous tick. My head would jerk suddenly and uncontrollably, which was strange and really freaked me out. It became quite embarrassing when it happened during conversation.

Though it never caused me to fall or get hurt, I also had an issue with feeling faint. However, the fact that I never actually fainted did not prevent me from developing a deep fear of it happening. I often had intense moments of lightheadedness that seemed as if I would lose consciousness. Many of the horrible symptoms that once only plagued me right before, during, and immediately following the attacks had blended themselves into the rest of my life.

Somehow, I managed to continue working through it all without many interruptions to my productivity. Thinking back, I am not sure how I accomplished it, beyond sequestering myself within an office. When my coworkers would go out to lunch for someone's birthday, I formulated an excuse about why I could not go. I shut my door a lot and spent my breaks and lunches browsing the internet in search of a solution for what plagued me.

I even read the Bible… the entire thing, in a matter of months. I figured that even if there was no specific answer in there to tell me what to do, God would be pleased with my efforts. I felt I needed to put in an equal effort to make Him happy with me rather than focusing on my own issues and incurring any more of His wrath. In my mind, I had done plenty to deserve his anger at times. I had no concept of His Grace. My view of Him was that He was easily displeased and quick to punish.

Feeling desperate and hopeless at times, I was only spurred back to life by the feeling that somewhere, out there, was a remedy for my pain and suffering. I won't list every single diagnosis I came up with, because there were far too many. Likewise, the number of remedies I attempted was a large number. Suffice it to say, I diagnosed myself with systemic yeast overgrowth, mold poisoning, demonic possession, various allergies to foods and airborne substances, some sort of chemical imbalance, and a rare digestive disorder, all to no avail.

Finally, I reached a point in which I sought medical advice. I was prescribed several different medications over a period of time. One was for ADHD, another was for depression, and another was specifically supposed to alleviate anxiety and panic attacks. One of the medications made my symptoms far worse. It only took a matter of days before I had to come off. Another prescription made me feel like a zombie, tired beyond belief and disconnected from the world in which I shuffled through.

I settled on one medication that did help in the midst of a panic attack. It calmed me down, with the only tradeoff of making me very sleepy. It did not alleviate the general anxiety that I felt each day, but at least I had something to turn to in the middle of one of my attacks. They would wipe me out, but I could finally escape. However, this wasn't a medication my doctor felt comfortable leaving me on long-term. It was highly-addictive, so another one was prescribed. After being on it a little while, I had an incident in which I decided this medicine wasn't helping me like I needed.

It was at the conclusion of a particularly long day at work in the parking lot. As I walked to my car, I looked down at my keys, sorting through them to find the one to the car I'd taken to the office. As I went about my task, I heard the sound of a loud vehicle barreling down the road. I halted to watch a tractor trailer truck driving by. I watched it pass, as if everything were in slow motion. And in that moment I thought to myself, What if I stepped out in front of it? Answering my own question, I shrugged my shoulders, as if to say, *Whatever, who cares?* Those words from my past crept out with ease. This time, however, I bought into the idea of not caring like never before.

I then realized what I was saying to myself. It was particularly disturbing that I had no feelings about it one way or another. That's not how I was supposed to think of it.

The pills were not getting to the root of my particular problem, and in that apathetic moment in the parking lot at work, I finally realized it. I was not getting better. After abandoning yet another unsuccessful treatment, I found myself with more feelings of hopelessness. The doctor suggested I see a specialist, either a psychiatrist, a therapist, or both. The doctor's office didn't set up the appointment, so I chose not to follow up on it. I let it slide and went on my way, again trying to find an answer myself. I still wanted to be in control of it...whatever "it" was.

I knew my supply of special numbing medication would last only so long. I only had a limited amount of time to fix this before

I ran out and was back at square one. A time constraint is not a pleasant thing to experience when you already have issues of extreme anxiety and panic attacks. With the clock ticking, I became even more obsessed with my search.

It didn't take long before I felt that self-diagnosis wasn't the right way to address this. Instead, I decided that maybe I was not fully relying on God. I then sought the input of people I thought might be able to give me some good "Christian" advice. When you view God the way I did, His will seems so mysterious and out of reach. You feel like you can never figure out what He wants. The uncertainty creates even more anxiety.

I listened to many sermons, read religious material online, and talked to a few fellow Christians and ministers in person. For the most part, I related to a lot of what Job received from his friends in the Bible. According to what I was hearing and reading, I either needed to repent of some sin in my life, figure out and learn the lesson God was trying to teach me, or get back in His good will somehow.

I believed I was finally on the right path. I had been seeking help from everywhere, but kept coming up empty-handed. The idea of God withholding healing from me because of something I was doing wrong made perfect sense. I knew how messed up I was and had been in the past, with my many mistakes. Heck, I often replayed them over and over in my head, beating myself up constantly for the decisions I'd made and could no longer change. Why wouldn't God feel the same way? All of this lined up with my view of God at the time. Basically, "He's hard to please, so try harder!"

I needed to do something extravagant to show Him I was deserving of being set free from my trials. But what? That question carried me over to the next step in my life... one that would likely do one of two things: end in healing, or cause me to hit rock-bottom.

THINGS TO THINK ABOUT

1) It is amazing what suppressed issues, such as fear and shame, can do to our bodies. I had many "symptoms" of my unresolved issues. Have you ever noticed your own unique set of "symptoms" that indicate something is wrong? This can be anything from stomach aches, headaches, exhaustion, irritability, the drive to constantly be busy with something, irresponsibility, drug and/or alcohol abuse, obsession with sex/porn, the desire of feeling needed, cutting, over- or under-eating, obsessive-compulsive behavior, feelings of hopelessness, and of course panic and anxiety.

___

2) In the midst of a very difficult time in my life, I was in search for answers. Think of a time in your life that was difficult. How did you search for answers? Where did you search? Who did you talk to? What did you find?

___

3) I was continually let down by my search. Nothing seemed to work. Have you ever experienced something similar? How did you feel? What did you do?

___

4) I was convinced God was withholding blessings due to something I had done to displease Him. How do you perceive God when things are not going well for you?

___

(9)

Church Ain't Jiffy Lube

"HEADS BOWED AND EYES CLOSED," THE PASTOR INSTRUCTS FROM THE PULPIT. Without needing to think, I quickly comply with his request. I have been waiting for this the whole service.

I pray silently, *God, I have done everything I know to feel better. You know my plight and the healing I so badly want. God, please make tonight the night I can finally put all of this behind me. I just want to be normal. These attacks, the dizziness, all of this… it's just too much. Please ease my burden! Forgive me for whatever it is I have done! Or even make known what you want me to do! I don't feel like I can carry this weight by myself anymore! Please give me another chance! I will do better!* Tears well up in my eyes as I beg fervently for a gift I feel I need more than anything else.

God, I know you have waited for me to do what I am about to do. I am relying on You to fix this for me, once and for all. No more searching the internet. No more medicine and natural remedies. *No more staying at home instead of going out with my family for a meal. No more avoiding things like church and birthday lunches at work.*

The pastor is praying the usual prayer that goes along with piano music in the background. But I'm not paying attention to his words, as I contemplate the long walk up there to where he is, in front of the communion table. It's actually not that far. No more than 30 feet from my seat. At the same time, it feels like 30 miles.

It's almost that time in the service when the altar is open for people to go pray. After he finishes praying, the congregation sings a hymn. Then it will finally be the time of "invitation."

If I can prove I am willing to get up in front of everyone and do this, will You lift this burden from me? This has to be what You want... something big I can do to please You! God, please honor what I am about to do. Show everyone what you can do by healing me. Please show me what you can do!

The pastor finishes his prayer. He instructs us all to open the hymnal and begin singing. As the congregation begins the first verse, I'm glad God's favor is not dependent upon us all being in tune.

This is it. It's now or never. No sooner do I think it than my body seizes up. *Crap, I have GOT to do this.* I argue with myself for almost the entire song. *This must be the devil trying to keep me from pleasing God!*

The second verse rolls by. *If I wait much longer, the song will be over! I cannot miss my opportunity! Like the pastor said before the song started, this could be my last chance!*

I force myself to stand up after we begin the last verse of the song. I think sarcastically to myself, *I bet everyone is really happy with me, waiting until the very last verse to go up there. Now, they have to stay a little longer while the pastor prays for me. Why didn't I go earlier? Will my hesitancy be something God is displeased with?*

I make my way up to the front. The dizziness I feel causes me to stumble, but I finally arrive at the two steps leading up to the podium. These two steps serve as the altar. I kneel down. *My God, I am begging you… touch me tonight and heal me. Make me whole again. I know I have done nothing to deserve this healing.*

The pastor continues to stand at the front for a while, allowing me some time to myself. Then he turns and makes his way over to me and begins praying. I listen to his words—sounding more eloquent than mine. When he is finished, I tell him why I have come to the altar.

"Pastor, will you and the deacons anoint me and pray for healing?" This is something I have seen done my whole life for those who are sick or struggling with something. I have never done it before until now.

"Deacons, please come forward." The pastor motions for the ordained deacons of the church to congregate around me in order to pray. As they bow their heads, placing their hands upon me, these men have no clue as to what is really going on with me, but they do know I have been struggling for some time now. Only I know the intensity of this battle.

The deacons murmur their prayers for me. I cannot make out what they are saying, though I hear my name mentioned every now and then. It feels a great deal more comforting to have these men beseeching God on my behalf for Him to heal me. The more prayers I get, the better the chances I will be healed. To be sure a deacon's prayer is more valuable than my own!

Then the pastor begins praying. The speed of his words increases simultaneously with the gradual raising of his voice. It's one of those prayers that makes your hairs stand up, like lightning building up static electricity in the air. My emotions are stirred. I wait for something to happen. I expect a feeling of power to wash over me, cleansing my contrite soul and completely healing me.

After a few more moments, the pastor slows his speaking and ends his prayer, much like the climax of a song. "Amen." We all raise our heads slowly, taking in the feelings of the moment. Several of the deacons pat me on the back and nod their heads as if to silently say, "It is done." Everyone returns to their seats for the closing of the service.

As I make my way to my seat, I glance around, mentally testing the waters of my newfound freedom. *I cannot wait to live my life normally again! God, thank you!* I totally expect the dizziness, anxiety, and stress to which I have grown accustomed to be completely gone.

As I walk, I begin to notice something at the fringes of the euphoric feelings that cause my heart to sink. I stumble a bit. *Wait, it's still there! I'm lightheaded!* All of the symptoms of my struggle are still there. Nowhere is that feeling of freedom from my struggle. Nothing has changed.

Tonight, at church, I sought God's healing touch at the altar. I so desperately wanted healing from Him. Yet now that it is over, I feel the same as I had before. I am no different.

By the time I return to my seat, I feel flooded with emotion. I try to convince myself this healing might not be instantaneous, and that it might occur over the coming days. I no longer believe even myself. Instead, I feel a depth of hopelessness I've never experienced before, in all of my years. That trip to the altar was a last resort to fix what was wrong with me.

But now, as I look down at the pew in front of me while the pastor performs his final prayer, I decide to stop asking God for help. It seems obvious He doesn't care about my trial or how much I need Him. My fate in life is decided, and I am destined to struggle for its entirety. In my mind, I cannot count on Him. I am doomed to a life of panic attacks, debilitating anxiety, and faceless fears that cannot be overcome. *I am on my own. I am alone.*

My wife and I drive home after the service in silence. She is unaware of everything going through my head. I internalize everything, giving no indication about what has happened. Once we're back home and alone in the kitchen, I lean against the bar with both hands, and my head down. She asks me a question about something she had read in the Bible. I don't hear what the question was. But I can't contain the frenzy of emotions within me any longer.

"Who cares?!" I shout in response to Melissa's question. She steps back, eyes wide. She has no clue how to respond, so she remains silent for me to vent. The anger I stored up since getting back to my pew blows up. "Do not ever ask me a question about God or the Bible again! Ask someone else! I am done with it all! He's done with me, so I am done with Him! I went up there tonight, and I put it all on the line for Him, and what did I get? Nothing! He does not care about me, and you shouldn't either!"

My anger boils within, an uncontrollable tempest of rage and frustration. I tried everything to be the good Christian I thought God wanted me to be. Despite my fear of having a panic attack, I even mustered the courage to approach the altar in front of everyone. He did nothing to help me, and I am furious about it.

Why God? Why won't you help me? I just cannot do this on my own! I have tried everything to fix it, but nothing has worked! There's nothing left that I can do!

All of a sudden, I begin weeping uncontrollably. I gently release my clinched fists. Tears steadily stream down my face, dripping on the counter I am leaning on. *Okay, now I have really lost it. One minute I'm ready to punch a hole in the wall, the next I am crying like a baby. What the heck is going on?*

◆ SURRENDER ◆

I said I was done with Him, but I wasn't. Actually, I was finally doing something I had needed to do for a long time: venting to Him.

As I stood in the kitchen, I was finally being real about how I felt. Those tiny prayers I offered Him for months, all in an effort of trying to appease Him, were not authentic at all. Those prayers were all focused on getting Him to fix my problems. Never once did it occur to me that there was much more that God wanted to help me with... deeper things that were the real issue behind the mess I was in physically and mentally.

Although I did not realize it at the time, my trip to the altar had been one last attempt at controlling my situation by trying to get God to do what I so desperately felt I needed Him to do. After it failed, I was finally broken completely. I was at rock bottom.

At that point, there was a drastic decision to be made. Would I wallow in self-pity and begin an era of taking out my anger on myself and others? Would I go back to trying to find a quick fix? Or would I do something completely different than any of my previous tactics? God had finally guided me through the previous options for a reason. There had to be more to my experience than merely finding a way to ease the symptoms. After that night, I opened myself up to a long and winding path of self-discovery to finally uncover what was going on inside of me. I had no idea what it meant or where it would lead.

That night, I did something I had never done before. It was something God had been patiently waiting for me to do, as He knew I needed that first step before anything else could take place on my journey to freedom.

I surrendered.

I relinquished all control and abandoned my devotion to avoiding those things that caused me anxiety. I surrendered my devotion to the masks I created to hide behind over the years.

I surrendered the foolhardy and transparent efforts at pleasing God with "good Christian behavior." I even gave up the notion that I knew exactly who God was! At last, I was in a position to open myself up to the possibility of getting to know the real God.

It was terrifying to let go of control. I had no idea how God would respond. I had no idea what effect it would have on me. However, it was somehow a relief... a strange relief. I no longer expected a quick progression. I surrendered that expectation as well. Church was not like Jiffy Lube, where I could get a tune-up when I wanted and everything would be okay afterward. I made the mistake of approaching it like another one of my supposed quick-fixes. My focus needed to shift from an obsession with my symptoms to discovering what inside of me was causing them. It wasn't mold, or a rare virus, or a brain tumor. I accepted that fact. I would not find the cure to my problem on the internet. I could not depend on someone else to fix me. I knew this would require something more out of me. I also knew this would not be easy.

But how would I go about walking down this path? I had no clue how to navigate it.

THINGS TO THINK ABOUT

1) I was convinced I would receive what I was looking for when I sought it at the altar. Have you ever asked God for something and it seemed like you came up empty-handed? Did you feel He might not be listening or even punishing you? Do you have any unanswered prayers?

_____

_____

2) I experienced feelings of hopelessness after realizing my final attempts at a quick-fix failed. The word "depression" might accurately describe my symptoms as I approached the end of my efforts. Do you ever find yourself feeling like there is no hope?

_____

_____

3) When we feel hopeless, we can continue to attempt to find hope in our own efforts to control things, or surrender our efforts to be in control. The latter requires that we choose to blindly trust God in a way that we may never have. What might it look like for you to "surrender"? What would you have to give up control of?

_____

_____

4) I reached a point in which I accepted that the panic and anxiety might not be the root problem, but symptoms of something else. Can you think of a time in which you were likely focused on symptoms instead of attempting to address the cause of them?

_____

_____

_____

(10)

Someone Trusthworthy

As I drive my little green SUV north on Interstate I-95, I struggle to keep calm. Long drives are so difficult for me, but this is an important one. I am determined to make it. I should be about halfway there at this point.

The anxiety starts to build. I can feel it as I become a little disoriented. I force myself to breathe slowly and deeply to keep it at bay. As I approach Exit 102, I finally admit to myself that it's not safe to continue, as I am now becoming rather shaky and dizzy. The last thing I want to do is put someone else in danger, so I pull off the exit ramp.

At the end of the ramp, I pull over to the side of the road. *Neil, take it easy. You can do this.* I talk myself through it, trying to forget how anxious I am. I rub my head nervously. I need to do everything I can to avoid thinking the worst: one of these attacks could potentially end today's journey.

The drive to the counseling office today is a rough one. I am sure some people think it is ridiculous to drive more than an hour to see a counselor. However, I am ready for some help... some real help. Nothing will keep me from that now. I had to leave work early today to make it to the appointment. I probably will be doing this on a regular basis for a while, and I am okay with that. Thankfully, my boss is too.

After a few minutes of breathing exercises and attempting to distract myself with other thoughts, I feel more in control and able to continue the drive. I merge back into north-bound traffic and press on. Thankfully no other attacks occur and I reach my destination with time to spare. Though I am no longer dizzy, I still feel stretched thin and I excuse myself from the waiting room to the bathroom.

I stand in front of the mirror in their tiny bathroom. I splash cold water on my face in an effort to calm my nerves. I am still anxious... very anxious. My hands are shaking. I can hear myself trembling when I take a deep breath. What I am about to do here is potentially a real step toward making progress on understanding my problem and fixing it.

God, you have brought me here. After years of living in fear, I'm here. Whatever you want me to learn... whatever you want to show me... I'm ready. My submissiveness still surprises me. It doesn't feel natural, due largely to spending so many years fighting to control every aspect of my life.

The cool water feels good, but I need to be ready when I'm called. I wipe my face with a paper towel, though I barely have room to move in this little space. I find it ironic that a counseling office would have a bathroom small enough to aggravate anyone with even a remote case of claustrophobia.

Alright God, here we go. I walk myself out and back to the waiting room. As I sit, the jitters really set in. I have tremendous trouble just sitting somewhere, waiting. It's not as bad as waiting in line at a superstore, but the feeling is quite similar. The lady behind the desk has such a relaxing tone when she speaks to people on the phone. When I checked in earlier, that same voice felt soothing to me.

Seeking counsel is something I have avoided for a long time. Yet now I am desperate, and my desire to get to the bottom of my issues overshadows my fear of the unknown, which this largely is.

In the days following my experience of the altar service not meeting my expectations and the explosion with my wife, I spent much time throwing myself at God, hoping something would stick. I read the Bible every day when I had free time. I listened to "Christian" music, which is somewhat painful at times since some of the art labeled "Christian" is not so great. I jumped headfirst into Sunday School discussions at church, often not wanting the conversations to end. I imagine that God found this sort of behavior rather amusing because I was obviously overdoing it a bit. He may not need it, but I did. He has used this time to do something important for me.

The experience has only served to solidify my surrendering from being obsessed with the symptoms of fear, anxiety, and panic that haunt me. While those things still continue to hound me, I am learning more and more about how to live my life without those things being my sole focus.

As is often the way of God, I accidentally stumbled upon a way to get help. It's funny how we often won't find what we need until we quit trying to get what we want. In a conversation with a friend, I was given the idea of contacting someone who specialized in something called "Christian counseling." My focus of late has been to replace everything in my life with a "Christian" version of it, so this sounded intriguing. Not only do I stand to benefit from the Christian focus, but I also gain the advantage of their professional training in counseling and this individual's ability to marry the two together to help people with issues like I have.

PANIC TO PEACE

The friend I spoke with is named Lizzie. I actually knew her, because she is married to Anthony... the life-long friend who escorted me onstage at the Beta Club induction back in high school. Lizzie directed me to the counseling I now await. When I learned that the trip here would be more than an hour long, I was rather concerned. I have difficulty driving anywhere at all, even if it is a few minutes down the road, due to the level of anxiety that haunts me and the always-imminent panic attack. However, I proved to be up to the challenge, because here I am in the waiting room. Again, my focus isn't completely on those things that debilitate me, though they continue to be a tremendous burden.

I am very early for my appointment, but this is typical of me. I do not like to be late, but when my anxiety is in high gear, that trait becomes even more pronounced. Being late draws attention to me, and that's not something I want.

I hear a door open. I hear the footfalls and voices of two people approaching the waiting room from down a hallway. One is female, whereas the other is male. Could this be him? I am anxious to finally see this guy. Is this someone who can really help me?

They suddenly enter the room. The man is dressed in a button-up shirt and tie with khaki pants and no coat. *That's him!* His tie is a little loose and crooked, probably from a long day of work. I have the 5:00p.m. appointment, which is his last timeslot of the day, so that makes sense. He doesn't look at all like what I expected. Okay, so he's not a "gotta wear a suit and tie preacher guy," which is more than okay with me. He actually looks like someone I would feel comfortable talking to. He walks the lady up to the counter so the receptionist can set up her next appointment. He then heads back to his office, or the restroom, I am not sure which. It's still another five minutes until my appointment, so he likely has other things to attend to before then.

Several minutes pass before he reenters the waiting area and approaches me directly. We shake hands and he introduces himself as Michael before inviting me to sit in his office. We spend some time chatting, just getting to know each other a little. My anxiety is bursting at the seams. Being confined to an office with all this attention on me is quite difficult.

"I am feeling a bit nauseated," I cautiously tell him, fully expecting a puzzled look from him. It doesn't phase him a bit. He casually grabs a trash can, sits it in front of me, and continues chatting. It's like he isn't weirded out at all by what I consider my usual bizarre, embarrassing behavior. His approach creates a strange sense of calm within me and my nausea begins to fade. I haven't been in a place with anyone in a very long time where I did not feel like I had to hide something.

He continues to ask me questions and genuinely listens to my answers. I begin testing him with some of my stranger symptoms and personality traits. Still, nothing phases him and he acts like all of this is perfectly natural. *What the heck? Is he for real?* He doesn't even act like he's feeling sorry for me either. He laughs at some of the stories I tell about my problems, but not in a condescending way. It's like he has experienced the very same things. It's like he understands.

❖THE POWER OF ACCEPTANCE❖

It was after that first meeting that I decided I was on the right course. Over the coming weeks and months, I continued to see Michael. That part of my journey was not easy. Coming to the end of one's self effort has the requirements of finally giving up excuses and making sacrifices. We must expect and accept those things on a journey to find true help for our struggles, which I discovered during that time.

I put forth a considerable amount of effort even to make the drive to each session. Despite looking forward to my appointments, I still had to pull off at one or more exits along the way to allow my anxiety to subside. I could only imagine what my boss and coworkers thought about my weekly routine of leaving early from work. But I put that out of my mind by focusing on the greater quest before me.

The first part of my time with my new friend, Michael, was not at all what I expected. It wasn't so much about the techniques he used to teach me how to handle my anxiety, panic attacks, and other issues. I did not realize it at the time, but these initial meetings became more a matter of feeling his unconditional acceptance of me. The man would not budge, even when I shared the horrid things that I had done in my life. That gave me the confidence to make sure he heard it all, the good and bad.

Experiencing this level of acceptance was a key in finding the truth about my fears, anxiety, and panic attacks. At the same time, this acceptance opened the door to much more important truths. To my surprise, I discovered that much of what I believed before meeting Michael was not true, but I had lived most of my life convinced that it was.

I believed that there was something fundamentally wrong with me and that I should be ashamed of it. I didn't believe anyone would accept me if they knew the "real" me. The rejection I received in life from several key moments was something I had taken to heart. I felt completely justified in thinking this way about myself. This view of myself then carried over to how I perceived God looking at me. Sometimes I believed He saw me the way I saw myself, and I needed to work hard to change for Him to accept me. At other times I believed no amount of effort on my part could ever be enough for Him to change His mind about me.

I believed I was a failure. From the moment I stood on that stage in 8th grade and bombed that speech, I was convinced of it. Once again, what I believed about myself revealed what I believed others thought about me, including God and anyone else in my life. Therefore, I believed others saw me as a failure too, and that God was disappointed in what He saw when He looked at me.

I believed I was crazy. I sincerely felt that, at some point, I had lost my mind. I saw the looks people gave me when they learned about my struggles with panic and anxiety. And those few times when someone saw the symptoms for themselves, I was even more convinced that I was nuts. I assumed I knew what everyone thought of me. In my mind, they thought I was a weirdo and the best I could get from anyone was for them to feel sorry for me.

But after attending my first few sessions with Michael, he defied my every belief about myself, others, and God by how he treated me. This experience opened the door to me being able to reconsider those beliefs. Michael did several important things to begin the healing process for me.

First of all, as I have already mentioned, he accepted me, plain and simple. Through the simple power of conversation, he exerted a substantial amount of energy that made me feel rejuvenated and uplifted. But, most importantly, he listened. He really listened. He sincerely wanted to hear me and understand me. Even despite the worst stories I could throw at him, he responded with kindness and understanding. He looked past my jaded exterior and saw my true worth and potential. He trusted there was something in me that I did not think existed.

Michael believed in me. Where I felt downtrodden due to failures in my life, he was encouraging. He did not define me by my failures. He did not, for even a second, believe I was crazy either. He treated me with respect and held only the expectation that God would reveal what I needed during our time together. He had hope for me, and it was highly contagious.

Acceptance helps peel our masks off. When we finally take them off, not only do others get to know the real us, we get to know ourselves too…perhaps for the very first time. Acceptance also opens the door for us to reconsider our false beliefs. It gives us the confidence to question our views of ourselves and even

God. When I saw Michael could believe in me, I began to think, "Maybe God hasn't given up on me."

Over the course of the first few weeks as I came to trust Michael, the mindset I brought in with me began to fade, particularly my misperceptions of myself and God. I did not even realize it while it was happening. While we had a professional relationship in every sense of it, the core to this experience was the same as any healthy relationship. It had a foundation of trust.

We all benefit from a relationship with someone who is trustworthy, accepts us, and listens to us. It's risky, though, as people often let us down. However, it is worth the risk. When we find them, such relationships encourage personal restoration and healing. God knows it to be true. He spent a lot of time and energy in restoring our relationship with Him through Christ, and the realization of that relationship has supernatural healing qualities, including giving new life to us. The more we trust Him, the more we feel able to open ourselves up to Him, sharing both the good and the bad. The more we do this, the more Grace we receive from Him, with all the acceptance we will ever need.

The next phase in this journey was upon me. I continued my meetings with Michael, realizing the blessings they were in my life. After challenging my personal beliefs about myself and God, it began to become clear what my issues stemmed from. I was finally starting to understand why I struggled so much with fear, anxiety, and panic attacks.

THINGS TO THINK ABOUT

1) Acceptance is a crucial need that we all share. Feeling unaccepted, I encountered many struggles along the way. I benefitted greatly from meeting someone who accepted me as-is and then opening up to that new friend. Do you have someone in your life that you feel comfortable sharing your feelings with when you are struggling?

_____
_____

2) If you have someone in your life that you can trust, but do not open up to them, what is holding you back? If you do not have someone, would you be open to seeking such a relationship with someone? Why or why not?

_____
_____

(11)

Sunday Message

"So, we're not going to church today?" My wife asks one last time before she commits to another activity. She is already dressed in her exercise clothes.

"No, I just don't feel up to it today," I say. "I will just watch a sermon on TV, listen to a podcast, or something."

She nods with a look of understanding. She knows what I mean by that. My anxiety is rather high for some reason today. I don't think I can sit through a service at church without a panic attack setting in. I'd end up missing the entire sermon because I'm too busy focusing on breathing and not passing out. She wanted to give me one last chance to change my mind. But she does not push me. Although she's had her moments of frustration, it's still unbelievable to me how patient and kind she is to me on a daily basis. A lesser person would have knocked my anxious head off my shoulders by now!

"I'm going to go run on the treadmill a while," she says as she heads for the door. I smile and wonder why she even bothers with a treadmill. It's always a workout for me just to keep up with her. A trip to the grocery store is like a marathon. She's a busy lady. That, and she walks incredibly fast wherever she goes.

"Okay," I respond. As she steps out to the garage where our treadmill is, I turn on the TV. Since I'm going to miss church today, I am going to see if God wants to talk to me through some other medium, whether it is a book, sermon downloaded on my smartphone, working out, or reading the Bible to myself on the porch. They're all possible ways for me to connect with Him. I have been doing this for a while and have discovered such activities quiet my mind and offer a chance for me to engage and wrestle with spiritual truths. As for today, TV will suffice.

There is a minister beginning his sermon, an individual whom I've listened to on multiple occasions. A preacher on TV whom I actually listen to is rare. It's just not my thing. He is different for some reason. I have enjoyed listening to him at other times, which contributes some to my decision to listen further. I do not want to miss opportunities for God to speak to me. If I am going to listen to any guy on TV, he will be the one.

Though I've never attended one of his services in person before, I have grown to respect him. He is a great teacher. He is older and speaks with obvious wisdom and humility. I can tell this by how he shares his own experiences with living out his faith in God. He is not like some pastors I've known and heard speak. He doesn't rely solely on telling the congregation how they should be ashamed of themselves, reminding them that they are all definitely headed for hell, and reinforcing how they need to work harder to please God in order to get a response of some kind from them.

Today, this pastor is encouraging listeners like me by sharing insight into the spiritual gifts God has given each of His children. *I cannot believe this...* As he speaks about one gift in particular,

I struggle to fight back tears. I am mesmerized by what he says. Every trait he shares about someone with this gift...they are descriptions of me! *Every single one of them is me! This is unbelievable.* It's as if he has me visualized in his mind and is speaking directly through the TV to my harried soul. I realize I am now on my knees.

I'm not a complete failure!? As if the gates of heaven open and clarity of thought rains down upon my tired mind, I realize there is truly something special about me. God has taken the time to give me a gift. He actually put effort into entrusting me with something seemingly important. *Why would You do that God?* There's one answer that immediately comes to me, from a higher entity entirely.

You are special to me, Neil. You are my son. I love you, and I have really awesome things planned for you. You have a purpose. I want to work with you and through you. This is just one of the ways I want to do that.

The validation I receive from this is overwhelming. Tears roll freely from my eyes, and I cry without control or restraint. A calming warmth flows over me, and I can literally feel the anxiety wash from my body. This is a moment that no one gets to share in except God and me. I kneel face down on the carpet in my den, oblivious to anything but Him and me.

❖UNEXPECTED VALIDATION❖

This message of validation was unexpected. God chose to speak to me through a pastor on TV, conveniently on a Sunday morning when I was so anxious I could not even stand the thought of going to church. Instead of punishing me for not going to church, like I used to think He would, He met me where I was: in the living room of my house watching television.

Even after a few months of meeting with my friend, Michael, my anxiety was still unpredictable. I had good days, and then I had bad days. Although the anxiety was continuously an issue, the panic attacks decreased in frequency. I attribute that obvious change to the fact that I had finally learned what they were.

Michael explained to me that, during a panic attack, my body was having a normal instinctual reaction. For instance, if a bear was chasing me, my body would react by releasing large quantities of adrenaline. This is called a "fight or flight" response, ultimately ensuring that I had the energy to run away and attempt to find safety. It also could give me the energy and strength to fight a would-be assailant. The body's response to such an instinct can result in many other physiological changes that are necessary in potentially life-threatening situations.

During a panic attack, my body was reacting as if there existed a stimulus worthy of that "fight or flight" reaction. However, there was none. When there is a bear, and a person has that reaction, they do not question what's going on. They would know full well what was occurring! But when I had that kind of reaction without a bear or any other perceptible stimulus, it made no sense. That scared me even worse. It led to all the confusion, the search for an answer, and the snowball effect of worsening anxiety and more panic attacks. My body had been overreacting and setting off the "fight or flight" response when I did not need it.

But why?

Michael helped me come to an understanding of that as well. For years and years, I stored up things inside myself. I hid behind false identities such as "I don't care" and "Super-Easygoing-Overachiever." I avoided things that needed to be dealt with: fears, hurt, and shame. My mind and body had had enough. I did not have room for anything more. My body was sending me a distress signal, loud and clear. It had sent other messages along the way, though they were more subtle and I did not take notice. But the panic attacks were something I could not ignore. For others who experience struggles similar to mine, panic attacks may not ever occur. We all have different "warning lights" that flash when something is wrong. However, one thing is for sure:

if left unchecked, whatever a person's warning light might be, it will eventually become so cumbersome something must be done about it.

When Michael helped me understand these things, the attacks became significantly less terrifying. The unknown was now known. The snowball effect was stopped. When an attack assailed me, it was still extremely uncomfortable, but it no longer provoked the kind of reaction I had before when I didn't know what was happening. I finally knew the truth about the attacks. I was not dying, for one thing. That was huge. So, the fear of death was no longer my primary concern. I also knew that all my other explanations of what was causing the attacks were bogus.

With the mystery of the attacks solved, it became a matter of addressing the mystery behind the anxiety in general. Those symptoms were extremely bothersome as well. What all had I avoided? What was festering inside of me?

Treating the symptoms was no longer my greatest concern. I was primed and ready for God to address root causes. Learning how I could trust Michael carried over to me learning to trust this God I thought I knew. Truthfully, I hardly knew Him. He had always terrified me, so I had mostly tried to avoid Him other than when I felt I needed to try to please Him somehow. But with the acceptance I now found through Michael, I had also begun learning how to allow God to accept me. He already had, but I just could not believe it immediately with the views I had of Him and myself.

The lens through which I perceived myself left me with a truly horrendous mental picture. This lens was crafted from the outcomes of many of my experiences in life. Long before the speech in the 8th grade, I had encountered things in life that whispered to me how messed up I must be. It all just did not take hold until later. From that speech in 8th grade to almost flunking out of college, the messages became clear. I bought into these messages, believing I was an utter failure, an idiot, and completely messed up. In my eyes, I was downright worthless. With that perception, my fears of failing, looking stupid, and being rejected grew and grew over the years as I had more experiences that seemed to validate this mentality. The lies we believe about ourselves are not something we just hear in passing. Instead, we experiences events throughout our lives that vindicate our flawed beliefs, and all the while, we often do not notice what is happening.

Without realizing the fallacy in my own thinking, I attributed my self-view to the one whose view matters most. I believed wholeheartedly that God agreed with my assessment of me. I viewed Him as looking down on me and shaking his head... so disappointed, and quite often angry with me. This is something we all experience. It is impossible to separate our self-view from our God-view. Our perceptions of everything, including ourselves, are hints at how we truly view Him.

My distorted core beliefs spilled over into my interactions with others. It wreaked havoc on my relationships. I learned to manipulate others rather than attempt at relating to them. The last thing I wanted was for someone to see what I saw in the mirror each day. I worked hard to avoid what I feared. I was obsessed with controlling everything in order to prevent being truly known. All of those efforts were stressful in themselves, and ultimately led to emotional distress over time. There were warning signs along the way... stomach aches, headaches, exhaustion, anger, frustration, and even my troublesome behavior. But I ignored them all. I let everything build up in the background of my mind, forcing my body and mind to work like a car that was running out of oil. I had no idea that a breakdown was imminent.

The emotional distress built up, leading to excessive fears, debilitating anxiety, and frequent panic attacks. I responded to this by chasing a cure for the symptoms. And all the while, my state of mind and body only worsened. I woke up to a different sense of reality once I reached a point of feeling hopeless. My only choices were to repeat the same cycle or surrender.

The moment of surrender opened up the door to a healing relationship that addressed my true inner struggles: the debilitating lies that tainted my perceptions about both God and me. My relationship with Michael that developed as a product of this was very helpful, but the ultimate blessing was the relationship God kindled with me through Michael. Through a trusted friend that truly cared about me and accepted me just the way I was, God began showing me who He was and what He saw when He looked at me.

And so I began to let God in. During my sessions with Michael, I didn't have to be perfect for him to accept me. Michael didn't even flinch when I shared what I considered to be shameful examples of things I had done, as well as things done to me. I did not feel like I needed to please him in order to be accepted. This experience caused me to give further consideration to something Michael suggested during a session. I began to toy with the idea that, because of my reliance upon His Grace through Christ, God was already pleased with me. If He really didn't need me to always do the right things and avoid every failure along the way in order to love me and be proud of me, then much of what I thought about Him was wrong.

I began to see God speaking to me in a variety of ways, not just through Michael. Looking back, I now see He had been doing that all along, but I failed to notice because of my faulty view of Him. My own perceptions had clouded it all. I assumed many incorrect beliefs were based on truth, so I had no reason to open myself up to anything else. Once I realized just how plagued I was by these false beliefs, I finally began to hear and see the many other ways in which He was communicating.

I heard Him in the encouraging words and actions of my wife. I would not know love the way I do now if not for her. God used her to reach out to me, to reveal His love for me through the blessing of a patient and enduring companion.

Other times I would sing along with Him, listening to music on the way to work. I became a fan of a particular singer/songwriter by the name of Derek Webb; a man whose lyrics challenged me with truths I was struggling to explore and embrace.

My quiet time, whether on the back porch or sitting on my bench in the weight room—lifting weights remains one of the very few hobbies I enjoyed through these trials—was another part of my life where I began to hear Him. Anything that helped me slow down and silence all the noises of life encouraged me to actually listen to what He might be saying to me.

With my newfound curiosity regarding who He was, I had an eagerness to look for Him everywhere. There were always things posing as Him to watch out for. However, as I learned to recognize the truth based on what He said in Scripture, those imposters stood out like a sore thumb.

Through Scripture, music, wholesome interactions with others, and books, He began answering the deeply-personal and all-important questions that were brought up during my sessions with Michael. *Who are You God? Who am I? Am I good enough? Are You pleased with Me? Why? How are you pleased with me?* I began seeing God working through every medium to teach me who I was and who He was, even a preacher on TV!

I am not prone to emotional displays. Not now, and I wasn't then either. It's just not me. When I fell on my knees in front of the TV that Sunday morning, I am not saying that for dramatic effect. It happened. I had been asking God who I was to Him. That moment alone in my den at home was pivotal. God showed me something special. Not only was I accepted by Him, I was also deeply significant to Him.

God had many more "God-moments" planned for me. This was just the beginning of answering many questions about my identity and His as well. Even today, He is still answering.

This was not the finale, with regard to my struggles with anxiety and panic. Rather, it was a tremendous victory. It gave me hope. It also set the stage for me to have something I was not very familiar with at all: courage. I needed hope and courage as I moved forward over the next few months.

The unveiling, piece by piece, of the true identities of God and myself became a much needed foundation for what was to come. Without it, the battle I will describe in the next few chapters wouldn't have happened at all, or have been resolved in the way it needed to be. The truth was setting me free, while at the same time calling me to action. But to do what? Would it be enough? Would I truly find more freedom? Or would I just find out this was another false fix?

PANIC TO PEACE
THINGS TO THINK ABOUT

1) I discovered something astonishing. The views I held of God and myself were tarnished by past experiences. I was left with tainted images of myself and God that were not accurate. That ultimately led to fear, anxiety, and panic attacks, among other things. Have you ever considered that your views of self and God could be distorted? How might those distortions be affecting your feelings and behavior?

_____

_____

2) What do you see when you look in the mirror? What do you see beyond your physical self? Write it down. Do you feel rejected? Insignificant? Do you lack a sense of purpose? Describe yourself as best you can. Be honest. No masks. This is for you and no one else.

_____

_____

3) Draw a picture of God. Now, draw another picture of God looking at you when you have done something wrong. Is there a difference? Do you tend to see Him as you depicted Him in the second drawing?

_____

_____

_____

(12)

The Superstore

It's a Saturday morning, and my wife is getting ready to visit the local superstore for a few things we need around the house. She assumes that I will not go, as has become the norm. I haven't done things like that in a very long time. The fear of having a panic attack in such a public place always drives me away from volunteering to help. But this time...

Maybe I should give it a shot, I think to myself. The mere thought of it sends shivers up my spine. This is the first time I have even considered such a trip for as long as I can remember. I immediately begin arguing with myself.

Think this through, Neil. A superstore is the epitome of all fears. It's a place that effectively incorporates as many anxiety-provoking experiences as possible. It's a big, open space filled with people. Shopping will not be quick and easy. You'll need to endure the constantly-building panic inside of you as you navigate the store and its people. And even when it's time to leave, you still need to get through the lines at the registers. It's as if they are designed to provoke anxiety and panic with no escape. Even if you run out, Neil, everyone will see you and think you are weird or crazy, and you will have done it all for nothing! Come on, man, you cannot do this!*

I catch myself. *Hold on a minute! This is the kind of garbage that has kept me at a stalemate with my issues for so long! I have got to face this at some point. Why not now? It will never be easy. Never! At whatever point I decide to face these fears, it will be a challenge. Why not start out with the biggest challenge I can think of? What's the worst that could happen? Even if I throw up and pass out, I won't die. Heck, even if I die, wouldn't it be awesome to go out in a tremendous act of courage? At least my last act would be in defiance of these horrendous fears that have controlled me for so long.*

Realistically, none of that will happen. The most likely scenario is I go in there, I have anxiety, we do what we have to do, and we leave. I think I am far enough along on this path that a panic attack might not even happen.

"Wait, Melissa! Let me get my shoes." I jump up from the couch and run to the bedroom.

"Huh? What do you mean?" she responds, uncertain of my intentions.

"I'm going with you," I repeat myself as I sit down to put on my shoes.

She stands there for a second, not quite knowing what to do. She smiles and approaches me. When I stand up ready to go, she hugs me. "I am so proud of you. I will be with you the whole time."

Those words are incredibly important to me in overcoming a trial such as this. God has worked diligently through my wife throughout our marriage. Building up the nerve to go through with entering the superstore is no different. When she said,

"I will be with you," she truly meant she would be there for me, no matter what happened. But there is more to it. That statement validates another pertinent truth I never really considered when dealing with my fears. I never considered God as being "with me" in the midst of my difficulties. I always felt He was off at a distance.

As we pull up to the parking lot of the superstore, I have a mixture of emotions. Part of me is excited. This is a big, big moment for me. I could stay in the car and that would be enough for today. Getting this far is a victory. Heck, even thinking about coming was a success. But now I am faced with the next step. *Can I actually do this?*

I sit there, rubbing my head nervously. My wife is silent, watching me closely as she waits for my decision. Neither of us says anything, but she knows what's going through my mind. Will I go in with her, or settle for the victories I've experienced thus far?

I look at her nervously. "Let's do this," I say with a budding confidence that surprises even me. She responds with a smile and squeezes my hand.

I get out of the car and face the building, pausing for a second to take it all in. Again, Melissa takes me by the hand. She waits for me to make the first move.

We make our way into the automatic doors at the front, and she leaves me for a second to fetch a shopping cart. I glance at the store greeter smiling back at me. *What in the heck is she smiling about? She is basically welcoming people to hell.* "It's great to see you decided to join us today! Come on in and enjoy our many torture devices! If you have any trouble, track down one of our many employees who are not properly trained on where anything is!"

We make our way up to her, and she smiles and greets us. I do not really listen to what she is saying, only to what I imagine she is thinking, *Welcome to a place where you will walk a million* miles to one side of the store only to find out the item is on the other side of the store. Then you get to walk all the way to the other side and discover it is out of stock. Have a great day, sucker!

I think my anxiety is provoking a little anger and a lot of sarcasm. Well, this battle doesn't have to be perfect! We continue past her. Peripherally, I can see my wife glancing at me, checking my countenance for signs of panic. She's wanted to fix this for me for a long time, but she now knows she can't. I feel panic coming on strong. I glance around at the large space, the multitude of people rushing around, and the long check-out lines. Overwhelming noises assail me from every direction. It's like someone is poking my brain with a needle through my ears. The dizziness and brain fog set in. The makeup aisle is only a few feet away, with no one on it, prompting me to make a dash for it. Melissa follows along with me, knowing full-well what this means.

"What can I do to help?" she says quietly.

"Nothing. Hold on a second."

I go into my head. It's time for another debate with myself.

Neil, see, I told you this was a stupid idea. Now you are trapped. This is terrible! You can't do this! You cannot stay in here! You have GOT to get out, or else!

I argue back. *Or else what? What's the worst that can happen? I've made it this far! This attack will pass and I will be fine. No one is watching and they will most likely not even notice a thing. Why should the opinions of people who come to a store in spandex or pajamas matter anyway?*

I bear down hard in order to focus on something I know to be true. The panic attack, with all of its symptoms, is raging. However, this time there is something very different. I am aware of something I have never noticed in the past when struggling through an argument with myself.

I am not alone.

My wife is here with me, and that is unbelievably important. Her loving, supportive presence once again reminds me that God is also standing there with me. All those other times, it felt like He wasn't there, because I didn't believe He was. But how incredibly wrong I've been! He's right with me even after I was sarcastic and angry just a few moments earlier!

This time, as I panic, I know the truth. I'm panicking in the presence of a Father who cares for me, is not going to leave me, is cheering me on, and believes I can do this. He does not see a loser or a weakling. Instead, He sees His son to whom He has given everything he needs so I can withstand this onslaught of fears while standing in this makeup aisle.

With that realization, I suddenly feel the panic leave me like a cold sweat after a fever breaks. The attack is actually dissipating now. All that's left is me standing in that aisle, propped up against a shelf.

❖ FEAR FROM A NEW PERSPECTIVE ❖

At this point in my journey, I learned to argue with myself. After discovering that I could not trust many of the reflexive thoughts that ran through my head much of the time, I began forming a habit of challenging them. Through my counselor and friend, Michael, God had developed in me a new foundation that helped me stand firm in my arguments against my old ways of thinking.

One might think Michael pushed me into facing my fears. Surprisingly, he did not. He did encourage me along the way, but he never told me what to do. His confidence in me was motivational. It taught me how to see God in a more truthful way. God was not waiting for me to screw something up. He was not ticked off at me for my failures.

God was, instead, encouraging me, kind of like he did with Joshua after he took over leadership of the Israelites when Moses died. Joshua was charged with leading the entire population of his people into a new land that God had promised them, which would require many battles. God told Joshua to not be afraid or discouraged. The key to conquering fear and discouragement was God promised to be with Joshua in everything he would face from that day forward. Joshua was not alone, and he needed to believe that truth to dispel fear. In Joshua 1, God reminds Joshua to "be strong and courageous" four times, knowing full well the strength He had instilled in Joshua. God also reminded Joshua three times that He would be with him.

God was reminding me, through Michael, of those same important truths. He wanted me to know how He viewed me. He saw strengths in me that I did not. He knew I did not believe the truth, so He spent a lot of time and effort reaching out to me, much like He did with Joshua.

With Michael not specifically instructing me on everything, I did not have a to-do list for overcoming my trials, completely contrary to what I expected. At times, I wondered how I would know what to do to move forward. However, as I embraced more and more truths about who God really was and who I really was, I began to feel a push. The truth was motivating me. My old ways of doing things made less sense under this new light of truth. That Saturday morning, as Melissa was preparing to go shopping, the push to finally test myself overcame the resistance my fears had put up for years.

Once again, God spoke loud and clear through a person who loved me dearly. Melissa did not pull me into the store. She did not guilt me into it by reminding me of all my failures and how I "should" proceed. She did not try to provoke me to do it with more fear, like by suggesting things would just get worse if I didn't conquer that store that day. She lovingly stood there and waited, eyes fixed on me, fully believing I could do it. Her view of me was the same view God had of me. His view had not changed through all the mistakes and blunders I made in life. I cannot say there have not been times where I have lost sight of that truth since then, but in that moment, I knew it was true and I believed it. I accepted the truth my wife unknowingly conveyed to me about who God was and who I was.

My body, same as my mind, had learned to respond with panic over the course of many years. As my mind was renewed with this confidence, my body would eventually respond and catch up. Michael had explained this to me, which helped me understand why the panic attack occurred at the superstore. My body was still trigger-happy when it came to panic.

Despite things not turning out just as I had hoped without a panic attack, in that makeup aisle that Saturday morning, something amazing occurred. I had finally learned a different approach to fear. Instead of fighting it or trying to avoid it, which only served to draw more focus to the symptoms and increase the anxiety and panic, I actually embraced it. At one point, I remember thinking, *Bring it on!* as I walked through the store. The level of confidence I had and believing I was not alone in my struggle was unexpected.

Somehow, fear lost its power when I embraced it in His presence, believing the truth of who He was and who I was. It was a whole new perspective. I equate it to how sin lost its power when Christ embraced it all on a cross. Because Jesus bore our sins that day He was crucified, when He died, the power of sin to define and consume our lives was broken. It's the greatest example of love in history. When we embrace that truth, we embrace the grace that comes with it. It becomes reality and we are forever changed. The grace comes through faith. It's sort of a mystery, but it sure is beautiful and freeing. The power of fear was diminished much the same way when I experienced it while trusting He was with me. The freedom I experienced occurred not so much through effort on my part, but through faith.

More moments like this would happen as the following months rolled by. Facing scary situations was vastly different when I experienced them with a God who I knew loved and accepted me, rather than a God who kept His distance because He was angry and disappointed with me. It was also different facing it as a man who knew he held gifts granted by His Father, not a scared little boy left to fend for himself. It was as if I could not lose. Even if I had failed in some way at the superstore, I was not a failure. My identity was more than what I did or did not do. The security I felt was growing with each step of faith I took, as I faced fear after fear knowing I was not alone, and security is the antithesis of anxiety. Whether they were large steps like entering a superstore or small steps like going to the mailbox, it did not matter as long as I was moving forward down this new path.

THINGS TO THINK ABOUT

1) For me, facing one of my biggest fears began with a simple thought of going to a superstore. Do you have a big fear you might consider facing? What is your personal "superstore"? How would you go about facing that fear?

_____
_____

2) I discovered a change in perspective with regard to what I believed about God and myself. This change became the foundation for courageously facing my fear. I discovered I was not alone and found security in that new truth. As you consider facing one of your own fears, what is your perspective? Do you feel alone?

_____
_____

3) I entered into my battle with the superstore with a new weapon: I had learned to recognize my old and self-defeating thoughts and strike them down with truthful thinking. As you think of facing one of your own fears, pay attention to the thoughts that go through your mind. Write them down. Examine them closely. Question them. Argue with them. Are they exaggerated? Is there any truth in them at all? Ask the big questions, like: "Who is God?" and "Who am I?"

_____
_____

(13)

Another Speech

I CANNOT BELIEVE I AGREED TO DO THIS. I am sweating profusely. Though I am also a bit shaky, no panic attack is looming. It has been a while since I had one of those.

Several months after my trip to the superstore, I was offered an opportunity to jump head-first into a pool of fears that dated back to my 8th Grade Valedictorian Speech. That's right, public speaking! I have been asked to share my experience with anxiety and panic attacks with a large crowd, sort of like a testimony to how God has worked in my life up to this point and is continuously working to free me from the bondage of all my fears. I was told the audience would include people seeking help for a variety of personal issues, including anxiety, so it would also be a potential opportunity to encourage others. I also saw it as another challenge and an opportunity for more freedom, as it was another set of fears to face, so I agreed to do it.

It's the night of the speech and doubt about my decision is hammering at my resolve. *Am I really ready for this? I mean, this is a pretty intense test to see if I have really come as far as I think I have.* I am sitting with several other people at a round table. This feels eerily reminiscent of the debacle at my 8th grade graduation. We're each given a turn to speak while others listen, and my turn is swiftly approaching. I have my notes in my pocket, which I've read at least 100 times.

All the lies are present, just like they were when I was 14 years old. *Neil, you cannot do this! You will screw this up. You will stutter. You will pass out. You will freeze up and not be able to speak. You will look like an idiot to everyone here. They will feel nothing but pity for you.*

I know I need to argue against these lies. It is hard to muster up the energy to prepare to get up there on that stage and deliver this speech. My fears are very real and intense. But thanks to a few challenges already under my belt, the truths are protecting me much more easily than they would have without the God-moments I have been experiencing. But something new breaks in…

It's perfectly normal to be nervous, Neil. You are prepared. Actually, you are over-prepared. People are here to hear your story, nothing more. You really cannot mess up your own story! Just be yourself, even if that means showing you are anxious. It's okay. Those that need to hear what you have to say will be comforted by your honesty and transparency.

Wait, did I just say that? That's a step above the truths I have been telling myself up to this point.

Before I can spend much time considering this fresh and invigorating viewpoint, I notice the person speaking on stage is introducing me. I get up and make my way to the stage.

Once onstage, I pause for a moment and look around. The familiar lies are screaming at me from all sides. I see one lady staring at the ground. *Is she uncomfortable because of how anxious I look?*

Neil, she is like you. She is afraid. She is hurting. She cannot bear to look up because your story is her story, or at least very similar. She needs to hear it. Now, quit worrying about all these people and focus on Me. I love you, and I love what you are doing here. You will do great! Just keep going!

I know this isn't me simply talking positively to myself. It's more than that. I can feel a strong presence about me, one that buoys me up and makes me realize that I can do this.

I take a deep breath, look down at my written speech, and begin speaking.

Many things are different tonight than they were back in the 8th Grade. There are more people at this event than there were back then. Many more, actually. There must be more than 1,000 people surrounding the stage. There probably aren't nearly that many, but there might as well be because that's how it feels! For this speech, things are different in that I'm older and I have personally written everything myself. But the greatest difference has to do with my perception of the whole thing.

Not only do I know now that God is with me, but He approves of me being here and doing this. He is watching, listening, and beaming with pride as I force myself through the first few lines, too scared to look up. Several times when I dare to look up, I am immediately tempted to focus on what people might be thinking. But I don't. I, instead, focus on what I now believe He is thinking.

❖ FOCUS ON THE TRUTH ❖

There was no adlibbing that night during the speech. I did not deviate from my notes. I looked down at them more than I looked up. I did not walk casually around on stage, or entertain the crowd with hilarious jokes. I still wasn't a professional speaker, by any stretch of the imagination. But I did not rush. I did not look for an easy way out. I was nervous, and I showed it. But I was me, and

I was okay with that. And surprisingly, the audience was okay with it as well.

The demons you cannot see are far worse than those you can. While the outward symptoms, such as the panic attacks, dizziness, drug use, and even the "I don't care attitude" were bad, the lies beneath all of those surface issues were the fuel to the fire that tortured me for so long. I believed them so fully that they became part of me, and you cannot run away from yourself. And running away from your fears is, essentially, attempting to run from yourself.

For a period of time after the big God-moment at the superstore, I went on the offensive, looking for opportunities to do things that I would have avoided out of fear before. It became very obvious that God was at work in His relationship with me. Just as I had learned to act on the lies old experiences had taught me, I was now learning how to act on the truth through these new experiences. When you are scared of as many things as I was, there becomes no shortage of chances to face your fears. I had opportunities to exercise my new perspective on a daily basis.

Despite the momentum I built, there were still opportunities I passed up. I did not always take God up on chances to challenge myself and experience His blessings in new ways. For those moments, my internal battle was to refrain from beating myself up. I did not want to be defined by imperfect decisions, behavior, or even the occasional backing down from a fear-provoking situation. My identity was set in stone when God chose me to be one of His own. This did not stop the accusations inside my head from still being intense:

Neil, you are a stupid idiot. Just shut your mouth before you say something foolish.

I am not an idiot. God says I have "the mind of Christ". That's far from stupid. And I am just nervous right now, which is normal and okay. I spoke incorrectly. Big deal. I do know what I am doing.

Look at how you chickened out. You are a coward. You haven't changed a bit.

I am no coward. In fact, I am quite courageous in that I have not given up.

Over time, it became obvious that the arguments I engaged in with myself seemed to be different. The old lies and accusations that had held me prisoner for so long were becoming downright nasty and more pervasive. It was as if an enemy were planting these thoughts, and increased the intensity of the attack when I began to focus on the truth. In fact, that was exactly what happened during the speech about my experience with fear that I delivered.

I had learned that ANY truth was sourced from my Heavenly Father, whether it was truth about Him, me, or anything else. On the flip side, anything that disagreed with Him was a lie, and lies are always sourced from Satan, who I have come to know as "the Enemy". The Enemy had been planting lies throughout my life as I experienced hardship, humiliation, shame, failure, and rejection. After I believed them, he did not have to do much to keep me in bondage. All he had to do was give me occasional reminders and I ran with it. "Neil, remember that you are an idiot," he would say. "Oh yeah, that's right," I would reply, not knowing what was happening. I was being lied to, duped, and manipulated.

Once I began believing the truth and using it to filter out the lies, the Enemy had to work harder. Life offers plenty of opportunities for a well-placed lie to take hold. Many of these took place in my personal experiences, which I've shared in previous chapters. However, these moments of weakness did not stop even after I learned how to capture my thoughts and force them to obey Christ (the Truth), as Paul described in 2 Corinthians 10:5:

> We demolish arguments and every pretension that sets itself up against the knowledge of God, and we take captive every thought to make it obedient to Christ.

When I began seeing the game that was being played against me, the lies only got louder. Spiritual warfare isn't a joke! It was tiring. It was difficult at times to keep up the fight. Although my internal arguments were a great place to start, I began to learn that such a strategy may not always be the best way to finish a fight with a lie.

Through several experiences, I saw that I had much more success when I exclusively chose to focus and act on the truth instead of arguing against the lie and justifying my actions. I often seemed to get side-tracked during these arguments because my focus was on the lie, and the Enemy has all the time in the world to argue his case. And it's not like he is going to admit he is wrong. An argument with an opponent who will not make concessions can lead to a long, exhausting back-and-forth interaction that prevents any semblance of progress toward the truth. I could not simultaneously focus on the lie and the truth, so I found myself tricked into short-term bondage while even in the midst of an argument! The key was to move on once I had identified a possible lie. After that, my focus needed to be centered on finding the truth or believing the truth I already knew.

Knowing and believing the truth acts as an automatic filter. For example, if I know a jellyfish can hurt me, when I see one out in the surf, I do not go swimming around it. I do not bother listening to those around me who might say it is perfectly safe to go in the water. I go on to do something else at the beach... build a sand castle or something. Why waste time arguing with those around me, trying to convince them they are wrong? It only serves to hold me captive there, instead of enjoying other more wholesome activities. Perhaps others will even choose to follow me, once they see me going in a different direction, away from danger.

When I know and believe God's truth, anything that contradicts it really stands out. Arguing past the point of identifying a lie often only created doubt in my mind about the truth I already knew.

With my focus on the lie, I became distracted from the truth and it became easier to be swayed away from it.

My focus for many years had been on the lies and the fears that I had. Back in that superstore, on the makeup aisle, my focus shifted from all those distracting issues to fixate on a God I had not known well before. When focused on Him, I was focused on His truth and His Grace. In the presence of Him, the lies were obvious. Through experience, I got better and better at recognizing the lies and quickly reverting my attention back to the truths I had learned about God and myself. That night at the banquet, my second attempt at a speech further solidified those truths for me.

During that particular part of my journey, I applied the truths that I was learning by doing many of the very things I avoided for years due to fear. It was not easy. It was not a short season in my life, either. Replacing old experiences and beliefs with new ones took time. Although it was challenging in every way, including my patience, it was an exciting journey. Every day offered a chance at finding more freedom. Of course, I did not always view it that way. Some days I wanted to give up. The battle for my mind was and still is a bumpy path at times, which is a good thing. When it's not, I am likely not fully engaged in the battle.

Once a year and a half had passed in this incredible series of events, Michael and I decided we no longer needed scheduled meetings. I was walking on my own fairly well. He had imparted to me the knowledge of what spiritual warfare looked like. I knew now how to fight. The next step of faith was to jump out of the nest and attempt to fly. Certainly, I had cultivated a great friendship over the time Michael and I had together in sessions, and it continued afterward. Michael never saw himself as better or above me.

Many battles were won during that transitional time in my life. My life was changed in a phenomenal way. Everything even looked different to me: God, my family, my work, and even my face in the mirror. Due to radical experiences like mine, one might believe we can all conquer something once and for all in this life, never to be faced with it again. If ever that is true, it is quite rare. The Enemy does not simply give up. He continues to exploit our weaknesses and seizes new opportunities to trip us up with old and new lies. We must be prepared to argue back, but more importantly focus on the truth.

The next phase of my journey would bring to light something that would further aid me in the battle. The truth was vital, but there was more that God wanted to reveal.

THINGS TO THINK ABOUT

1) Even after some break-through moments in facing my fears, I did not seize every opportunity that came to me. When you have progressed in your own personal battles, how do you respond when you encounter a setback? What do you say to yourself?

_____

_____

2) Write down some of the lies you tend to believe about yourself. Think about times in which you faced failure, rejection, shame, humiliation, or some other difficult circumstance or interaction with others. For some, it helps to simply look in the mirror and write down what you see.

_____

_____

3) In Ephesians 1, Paul uses many words to describe the believers in the Church of Ephesus. Compare the description you developed for yourself to how Paul describes God's Children in the Church of Ephesus. Do you find any similarities? What's different?

_____

_____

_____

4) Do you ever feel like God is distant and waiting for you to do something more for Him to earn His approval? Read Ephesians 2:8-10 and Hebrews 11:6. They focus on the one thing God desires from us. What truly pleases God is when we trust Him (focusing on and believing the truth over the lies). We are often fooled into thinking our position with Him is dependent on something we can do or avoid doing. The way He feels about us simply does not change, even in the midst of our greatest fears and failures.

_____

_____

_____

(14)

More Than a Mind Game

WHILE STANDING IN MY KITCHEN AT HOME, MY CELL PHONE RINGS. I recognize the name on the caller ID as a friend of mine. He also happens to be a deacon at a local church. After a few minutes of small talk, he says something shocking to me.

"Last night, we were having a deacon's meeting at our church," he says to me. "We were discussing the need for a Youth Pastor. Your name came up."

"What?" I respond with a level of surprise that probably sets him back a bit. "My name came up? How did that happen?"

"Well, we were discussing it, like I said, and someone mentioned that you might be a good fit for our youth considering the challenges you've faced and overcome. It would serve as an excellent example for our youth to identify with," he responds.

I am absolutely astounded. I still feel like this is some kind of mistake. Why would my name even cross their minds for such a position? I gather myself and say to him as diplomatically as I can, "I am very shocked, as I was not expecting this. I will need some time to pray and think about this. Is that okay?"

"Sure, just let us know after a few days," he replies.

I hang up the phone and proceed to spend days thinking about this invitation. I really want God to tell me what to do. I receive no burning bush experience or writing on the wall.

After several days and much deliberation, I realize God does not seem to be providing much help. He definitely has not given an answer to what I should do. I finally decide to look at it as another way to face my fears, and I accept the position.

Several months pass as I settle in as a Youth Pastor. I love the teenagers that are in my group. They're awesome. They're also very forgiving and patient with me as I figure out my role, making mistakes along the way.

I have known the head pastor since long before I began working at the church. It is a very small community that we live in. Our relationship has gotten closer as we work closely together. One day, a conversation with him winds up taking a rather odd turn.

"We all need to know the name God has given each one of us," he says.

"What do you mean?" I ask. I know he has spent considerable amounts of time studying different names and their meanings. He often brings this up in his sermons.

"God has given us all names that hold deep meanings. It's another way of saying it is how He identifies each one of us," he responds. "The name he gives us is our true identity."

"Okay," I say, while I think to myself, *What does that mean? It sounds a bit mystical.* I really expected a better explanation or at least something I could easily apply to my own life.

Instead, the idea sounds quite odd. I know it may have some higher meaning and implication to it, but I can't fathom how that could possibly be of help to me.

But apparently God really wants me to take notice. See, this is not the only time I have heard this stuff about "names". This different, but intriguing choice of words has been mentioned to me before. Twice before, actually.

After hearing it this third time, I decide to acknowledge it as something important I should investigate, so I mention it to God in prayer. After all, if God is willing to work through preachers on TV, then He can work through just about anything.

Alright God, something about this concept must be important. I will open myself up to the possibility that You are trying to show me something. I will wait until I hear from You about it. I won't really be upset if I don't. But, if it can help me, I'm all for understanding the importance of my name.

As weeks, months, and then years pass, I almost forget about this whole "name thing" at times. I speak with God about it sometimes when I pray, but I mostly choose to focus on more pressing issues. I periodically read scripture and ask God, "Who am I?" and "What is my name?" in the hope for some kind of breakthrough. I find no answer for two years. That's right, around 730 days come and go before I hear even a whisper about this "tell me my name" thing.

After that long period of time passes, I just happen to go on a men's retreat with a few friends up in the mountains. The purpose of our getaway is to seclude ourselves from the outside world in order to seek to gain some greater closeness to God. As I study the scriptures for an assignment I was given by the leader of the group, I stumble across a passage:

> **For this reason I bow my knees before the Father, from whom every family in heaven and on earth is named**, that according to the riches of his glory he may grant you to be strengthened with power through his Spirit in your inner being, so that Christ may dwell in your hearts through faith-that **you, being rooted and grounded in love, may have strength to comprehend with all the saints what is the breadth and length and height and depth, and**

to know the love of Christ that surpasses knowledge, that you may be filled with all the fullness of God. (Ephesians 3:14-19, ESV, emphasis added)

My jaw drops.

I cannot believe this. God are you really finally answering me? I go back and read the verses again.

I reach the word "named," and once again, it's like a jolt through my body. *It really does say that. But is that you, God? Are you trying to say something to me here? I could be fooling myself. This could be nothing more than a coincidence.*

Immediately, I remember how God told Abram in Genesis 17:5 that He was giving him a new name. God was calling Abram into a bigger story at that point in his life, and it was as if He knew Abram first needed clarification on who he was to Him. Abram became Abraham. No longer did he need to be identified by any shame, guilt, or fear that he might have felt. The only thing that really mattered was how God viewed him.

I need a name change too!

The second half of that passage in Ephesians 3 nearly jumps off the page and slaps me in the face. "[...] to know the love of Christ that surpasses knowledge [...]." I let down my guard. This speaks directly to my wounded heart. *I need that, badly. I need something that's bigger than all this head knowledge that I've acquired!* I have been somewhat struggling with the truths I have been embracing, specifically because they often feel more like mere head knowledge than an actual identity that is real to me. I'm now even more convinced God is telling me something very important about who I am.

Several of the other guys on the retreat enter the room for just a moment, grab something, and leave. However, as I lay on a bunk bed in the corner reading, they might as well be invisible. I'm in another world.

My eyes dart back and forth, reading and rereading. Two words jump out at me over and over, "named" and "love."

❖ NO FEAR IN LOVE ❖

Three seemingly unrelated events in my life led to something much deeper that I had been searching for without even knowing it. A call and invitation from a friend led to a conversation with another friend. That conversation set me up for a special message from God at a men's retreat in the mountains years later. It's pretty amazing how God worked through all of this to get His message to me loud and clear.

After sharing my experience with panic attacks in front of a crowd, I had continued down the path of engaging my fears. That grew into a rather reflexive effort to run into fear rather than avoid it.

With time, my mind became open to new challenges. One of those was returning to school. I saw in myself the inherent desire to help others who were struggling, so I enrolled in a graduate counseling program. My wife and I took steps for me to resign my accounting position and go to school full-time.

It started out as a simple quest of exploration, really. I would take a few classes and see if I liked it, before returning back to my old career. I was not fully sure if my drive to become a counselor was based on some emotional response to all I had been through or founded on a legitimate desire that would last. And after one semester, I was convinced: I loved it.

During that first semester, I was approached by my friend, the deacon, who offered me a position as a Youth Pastor at his church. I left that conversation with all kinds of emotions raging through my mind. I had grown accustomed to advancing through my fears over the past year or so. However, I argued with God a little over this one. What in the world were these men thinking by asking me to take on such a responsibility? What was God thinking to plant my name in one of their minds in that meeting?

I was reminded by one of the truths I had learned many months ago: God had much more confidence in what He could do through me than I ever did. I spent a week deliberating over the decision. I needed to know what He wanted me to do.

I really sweated that one out. I didn't feel like I was getting an answer from him. I thought about how I was already taking a chance by going back to school. I just "tested the waters" by taking a few classes. I did not necessarily receive a direct answer from Him on that decision either. However, I was driven by the excitement of counseling classes. This position as Youth Pastor scared me in a way I'd never experienced recently. There was much more fear involved on my part.

So I decided to take a chance. I accepted the position. I told myself the truth, and I took a leap into the fear, just like I had done previously. Yet even as I made the decision, something did not feel right.

I quickly found out the problem was not in accepting the position. It was definitely no mistake. For a year, I served as a Youth Pastor and it was an awesome experience. I connected with terrific people, both young and old, in that church. What I experienced tested my boundaries, and God used it to grow me while serving them.

What haunted me amid all of this was that I knew there was something wrong in the actual process of how I made the decision to accept this position.

Something was missing.

Everything I had learned, not only with Michael but in all the ways God had communicated new truths with me, turned my life upside down in a good way. However, there was a piece of the puzzle I could not find. It was that one in the middle that really pulled it all together.

I began to notice over time that there was a mysterious missing piece. While I was experiencing many awesome things as I flexed my new-found freedom in life, sometimes the process of focusing on truth seemed mechanical. I knew a lot of new, wonderful things about myself and God. I was flooded with the new knowledge which consisted of a list of truths I had compiled about who I was as a child of God. They were really cool descriptions, but I had a difficult time connecting to some of them. The fears, though at bay, were still lurking in the recesses of my mind, and I knew it. I had tasted it, for sure, but my real freedom was incomplete for some reason.

Then, while at the men's retreat, I stumbled across Ephesians 3:14-19. That passage about God's love added a whole new element to how I would live from then on. It was not just about psychological ploys to trick myself into feeling better. There was more to it. Much, much more.

It was not just about being more positive about life. Positive thinking is just a mind game that only helps temporarily, at best. Positive thinking is not true spiritual warfare, because it often offers one-liners with no depth: "Oh, everything will be okay! Just try harder! Don't give up! Let go and let God!" Positive thinking is no better than negative thinking because it fails to address the core issue leading to the anger, anxiety, or depression in our lives. It serves as a delay tactic at best, putting off the real issues rather than addressing them directly.

If I wasn't careful, I could have easily treated everything I had learned as mind games such as positive thinking, legalism, or psychobabble. That day, sitting on the bunk bed at a men's retreat that I already felt was a total waste of time, I was divinely directed toward that missing piece.

Love.

This love that God wanted me to notice took all the knowledge I had received and blew it up into something much more tangible, relatable, and beautiful. It personalized all of my experiences. In fact, it was impossible to separate this love from God Himself. He and "it" were one and the same. And because He loves me, I am inseparable from it and Him as well.

That day, back in the superstore, as well as the night I shared my story of anxiety and panic attacks in front of all those people,

His love is what calmed my mind. His love was what gave me the strength to face those fears and push forward through them. Before zeroing in on that passage in Ephesians, I did not fully realize how His love was central to the whole thing. Without His love, the fears I felt would have eventually overpowered me, taking full control like they had so many times in the past.

That afternoon, while reading that passage numerous times from beginning to end, God gave me the missing puzzle piece. He gave me a name. He gave me the key to understanding my identity.

I was loved.

Living in the reality that you are unconditionally loved by God is a massive game-changer. I had lived most of my life believing there was no way He could love me unless I did something to earn it. Of course, I rarely thought I did enough for that to happen. The rest of my life I had spent "knowing" He loved me, but not truly experiencing it. I could quote the verses that stated this truth, but it was no more than flimsy head knowledge. God wants more for us than head knowledge, as Paul stated in Ephesians 3:19. His way of doing that for me was using three unlikely scenarios in my life to open up my eyes.

When embraced, this perspective of being loved changes everything. Not only does it give the confidence to face fears, it actually has the power to cast them out. 1 John 4:18 states, "There is no fear in love, but perfect love casts out fear. For fear has to do with punishment, and whoever fears has not been perfected in love." Finally, I was taking in what God wanted me to know more than anything: He loves me, and His love is more than capable of trumping any fears with which I might struggle.

All else would stem from that reality. This love was present despite all of my imperfections. It would challenge and further strengthen my trust in Him. All the arguments against lies needed to rely on that special strength. The truths I needed to focus on would only make sense in the context of a relationship in which

I was loved unconditionally. And when faced with enormous choices like whether or not to be a Youth Pastor, I realized He sometimes just wanted me to make a decision, as if to say, "Trust me in whatever decision you choose. I will love you either way."

THINGS TO THINK ABOUT

1) I had acquired a significant amount of knowledge about my own identity, as well as who God was. Then God dropped a bombshell on me. None of that was worthwhile without the fuel behind it: love. Do you see yourself experiencing this love God has for you, or might you be stuck in just "knowing" you are loved?

_____

_____

2) Try spending some time asking yourself the same questions I did: "Who am I? What is my name?" Stay with it. This may be something that takes a while. It did for me. God will make this crucial communication with you in a way that is just right for you to receive it fully. He may have already started setting it up with a series of events you have not even noticed yet.

_____

_____

_____

(15)

Warning Signs

I ROLL OVER IN THE BED AGAIN. For hours, I've been shifting and rolling to find a position that is comfortable enough to help me sleep. Agitated, I slam my hand into the bed. *Oops! I don't want to wake up Melissa.* I take a deep breath and try once more to relax. *It's just not happening. I'm not going back to sleep and I might as well get up.*

I look at the clock, which I've done every time I shift around. 3:14 AM. It's almost morning and I'm not sleeping. *It's going to be a terrible day. I will be tired the entire time I'm at work and even worse when I get home! A day down the drain!*

My issue of being awake during the hours of twilight is something I've struggled with from time to time. On several occasions, I've let this activity draw out for weeks before I finally acknowledged something was wrong.

Early waking is like my panic attacks, a warning sign. It is a symptom of anxiety for me. I have been feeling some of those familiar symptoms on and off for days, but so far I have ignored them. From slight dizziness, to a headache, to stomach pain… the signs are all there that something is wrong. But that isn't all.

Later that morning, additional symptoms begin to manifest. The first of these isn't mere agitation. The anger I feel is immediate, leaving me unprepared to cope with it rationally. Instead, I lash out at Melissa over something that has nothing to do with her.

"Whatever!" I yell and slam the door as I leave the house for work, cutting Melissa off as she is speaking.

I storm out to my car and throw my stuff inside. I hit my head on the door frame as I get in the car, a list of profanities escaping my control.

As I pull out of the driveway, my phone vibrates. I look down at it. Call from Melissa. I roll my eyes and ignore it. *I'll deal with it later.* I once again put off any introspection.

When frustrated like this, it is often tempting to just say, "You make me angry," pinning the blame on someone else. However, that only prolongs the issue and hurts others in the process. This morning, Melissa is the unfortunate victim of my failure to take responsibility for and deal with my problems.

The anger I feel does not abate during the day at work. I struggle to get through it without lashing out at my boss or coworkers. I notice the increasing use of sarcasm in my conversations, which is a telltale sign of inner frustration for me. Basically, it's a sneaky way to let out anger with less likelihood of someone noticing.

I feel like if I can just get home, I will be able to cope better away from everyone else. However, even in the time I have to myself when I get home from work, I find no respite. As I sit down to do some writing for the book I have started, I only feel an overwhelming desire to give up.

This is ridiculous. I stare at the computer screen, a word processing document open and a blank page staring menacingly back at me. *What was I thinking, trying to write a book? It's just not coming together. I should just give this up and not waste any more time.*

My mind is in a tumult and I can't focus on this simple task. I can only think about a recent counseling client who decided to discontinue our sessions together. *I am really messing up a lot of stuff right now. I need a break, badly. Maybe I should just quit for a while. I am not doing any good right now.*

I'm just reacting emotionally, but the sentiment feels so true that my life is truly hopeless right now. I hear Michael's voice in my head stating, "Feelings of hopelessness are yet another sign that something is wrong." They do not agree with the truths that I've learned about who God is and who I am as His child. I know, deep down, that things are far from hopeless. Right now, however, it does not feel that way at all.

My negativity suddenly surges inside of me. *Neil you are so stupid. Just admit it. You know you have no business writing on that pathetic blog you have, let alone writing a whole book. Come on! Grow up. Be a real man and find something else to do. This is ridiculous. That client left you because you screwed it up. You know it. It's not the first time either. Admit it. If you lay off all of this nonsense, maybe you will finally sleep like a normal person.*

As I watch the cursor continue to blink at the head of an empty page, it suddenly occurs to me. The anger, the sleepless nights, it all suddenly stands out as incredibly uncharacteristic of what is considered "normal" for me.

What the heck am I doing? I haven't been able to sleep through the night for days now. I snapped at Melissa, the person who has given me more grace and understanding than anyone I know.

And now I am considering the thought of giving up my passion for some of the most important things I have going on in my life!

I attempt to turn away from this mindset. In my mind's eye, I look about myself desperately for the truth to set me free from this mess. As suddenly as I look for it, it comes to me.

You're on to something, Neil. Something is not right. I've been nudging you all week because I knew you'd come around. Let's take a look at this together...

Neil, you have nothing to prove. You are just who I want you to be, and I am very pleased with what I see. Sure, you've reverted back to some old behaviors that you and I both know are not truly indicative of who you are as my son. But we are going to take care of that and you are going to be set free once again. I will do this as many times as it takes. There's no end to what I have with you. And look how quickly you catch yourself now? It's truly a miracle. Not only can you leave your house without the fear of a panic attack holding you back, you've returned to school and received a degree in something I have given you a great passion for. I am proud of how you are connecting with and helping my other children as a counselor. Remember, I have not asked you to fix them. Just love them, as I love you. You are doing well, my son. I will handle the rest.

I know this is true, just as I know I am not in the right frame of mind to continue trying to work on my book right now. I am exhausted mentally and I can't think clearly.

I decide to put the unfinished manuscript aside and address a more pressing matter. I walk into the room my wife is in and sit down with her to apologize. This apology is only the beginning. I also commit to taking note of all the warning signs I have had for a while now so that I can get to the root issue behind them before things snowball any further. Something is wrong and I need to make the choice to address it, or I will continue living the lie

I've fallen back into. The breakthrough in discovering the core problem begins the next day when my wife tells me she wants to go for an evening jog.

"Go ahead, I am going to watch a little TV," I tell Melissa.

"I won't be long," she says as she heads out the door for a jog.

As I flip through the channels to watch various programs, I notice the rug in front of the TV is dirty. This place needs to be vacuumed. I stand up, and proceed to vacuum the entire house.

Upon completing this chore, I realize Melissa has yet to return. How will she know I even did this? I really want her to notice the effort I've made! Maybe I will just leave part of the vacuum cleaner out, like I did it by accident. That way, she will see it and realize the work I have done.

I stop myself from this path of thought, which is noteworthy in itself. My lie-driven behavior is fairly sneaky. In many previous instances, this one would have passed by without my notice. But not this time!

What am I doing? Sure, having her approval would be nice, but I don't need it to prove I'm a decent husband.

This isn't the first time I've found myself seeking her approval. I have noticed I do that a lot when I wrestle with the fear of failure. This fear is one that routinely creeps up on me and leads to me feeling like a failure. Over the past few weeks that I've been struggling with sleepless nights and frustration, I have sought her approval numerous times through a variety of strategies.

All of the warning signs are symptoms that are connected. Up until now, I have done nothing about them other than try to ignore them, similar to what I did all those years with my fears until it all snowballed into extreme anxiety and panic attacks. However, this time I see a clear choice needs to be made. God is giving me a cool opportunity to embrace His truth, in that I don't need my wife's reassurances to feel better about myself. Additionally, dishonestly leaving out the vacuum as an attempt to manipulate Melissa is not the way to handle this. It would only be a failure to understand and appreciate my true worth.

Leave out a piece of the vacuum so she will know I've helped around the house by vacuuming, or put it all away and say nothing at all. The first option would grant me a greater opportunity to receive kind words from my wife. With the latter option, there's a good chance she will never know or say anything. I force myself to put the entire vacuum away in the closet. I sit back down on the couch, feeling antsy. *Alright Father, I am now going to have to rely on your validation here and no one else's. Holy crap this is hard! Now, I need to focus on the truth and refuse to make mention of this whole thing when she walks through the door.*

With a strong resolve, I sit back in front of the TV. I know I've made the right choice, as silly and mundane of a struggle it may seem. It's a small step of faith. No, for me, this is a huge step of faith! I finally rest again in the truth of who God says I am. I might just sleep better tonight!

❖IMPERFECTION & PRAYER CLOSETS❖

For about 2 years after the panic attacks began, God worked in many ways to reach out to me during my counseling with Michael. He worked through the people I was closest to and respected, like Michael, Melissa, my son, and others. He worked through scripture, songs, podcasts, and things I read. Past experiences programmed me to miss all of these inspirational messages and the grace He provided through others before that transitional time in my life. With my eyes opened to learning and applying the truth, the lies that held me hostage for so many years began to weaken.

For years after my counseling with Michael ended, I labored to reinforce this new perspective that God even now continues to weave together with me. As I write this book, I still feel His influence and watchful care over me. It has not always been fun or easy to endure the trials I've faced. Many times I have failed to hold onto what is true, and in those moments I've reverted back to my old programming.

When this happens, it can be very disheartening. It can make us feel that nothing has been accomplished along the way, as if we are back at square one. If not prepared for these setbacks, we can easily allow them to define us. One key to preventing this is to embrace an important truth regarding our imperfect behavior.

In the midst of my failures, God has shown me that He sees me as perfect in Christ even when I do not act like it. Part of having a healthy perspective on life, both physically and spiritually, is to understand and believe He does not require perfect behavior from us in order to love and accept us. From this, it's become clear that life is not about getting it right all the time. To believe otherwise is to believe a lie. When I've fallen for that trick, I find myself stumbling in my progress, beating myself up over small failures, and losing sight of the truths that have carried me to that point. In those key moments, it is critical that we remind ourselves that God wants only for us to trust Him (Hebrews 11:6). This understanding brings things back into the correct perspective. More specifically, it brings us back to reality. We must not trust in our own ability to perform well, because we will fail. Instead, we must focus on trusting Him.

I've found that catching myself before I fully slip back into old ways of thinking is a critically-important skill. I know my challenges will continue for the rest of my time here on this planet. By understanding the symptoms I regularly have that result from these trials, I can get myself back on track. If I ignore the signs, the old lies that governed my life return with frightening speed and the symptoms just get worse.

When I argued with myself at the computer as I first began writing this book, I was able to notice and acknowledge the signs of me acting on lies. It was apparent what was going on, and I had the choice to ignore the lies or do something about them. Once I did engage my truthful thought patterns, I heard the lies screaming at me as if to command my attention and distract me from my resolve. I recognized these thoughts as the same ones that enslaved me for years. In response, rather than relying on some motivational quote of the day, I grasped for a truth that contradicted those lies. Naturally, I reached for the relationship that had brought me out of the world of bondage I'd lived in before.

Regardless of what they might look like, when warning signs like anxiety, anger, or hopelessness appear, something is happening inside of us that is fueling them. These impulses are not, in and of themselves, the problem. They are merely what is seen on the surface, like an earthquake. What we witness above ground may be horrible and frightening, but what goes on beneath the surface is the powerful moving force behind it all.

It's very easy to get caught up in fighting the wrong battles when these symptoms show up. I chose the wrong tactics for many years. I dodged, avoided, lashed out, put on masks, and did anything else I could think of to fix the pain caused by my trials. After experiencing some crucial truths, I found myself able to pull away from that lifestyle more and more each day. Although my resolve has allowed me to take control over many things in my life, there were and still are moments when I slip back into my old habits. And each time I falter, the first step to a solution to these remains the same: acknowledge there is a problem.

After acknowledging the warning signs like my anger and sleeplessness, I engaged in the real battle, not with the symptoms, but with the thought patterns behind them. I began analyzing my thoughts, wherein I finally noticed the internal dialogue that had been going on for weeks. I had been ignoring these voices of conscience and acted simply on the powerful feelings I was having.

In the experiences I shared at the beginning of this chapter, God chose to use a simple chore like vacuuming to pull it all together for me. Times like that can be missed easily. To be prepared for moments like that, we need something to make us more keenly aware of what God might be saying to us. If we aren't prepared, we will likely miss it for a while due to the busyness of this world around us.

Finding a quiet place in life is always the key to calming one's mind from external and internal distractions. I grew up hearing my mother reference her "prayer closet." It was a place she could rest assured no one and nothing could interrupt her. I heard others talk about these as well, although it was not always a literal "closet." "Prayer closets" could be any place a person can close out the world and find mental clarity. One can get very creative with discovering his or her own "prayer closet."

In conversation with others, I've discovered that prayer closets are different for each of us. For me, one of my favorite prayer closets is exercise. Physical exertion often helps settle my runaway mind. It is in the midst of a grueling workout that I can usually find the peace I need to settle down the thoughts running rampant in my mind so that I can capture them, one by one, and refocus on a much needed truth to replace them.

When I cannot run or lift weights, I listen to music. It's another prayer closet. During some evenings, I use both exercise and music to buoy up my efforts further! I have several go-to songs that naturally hit on messages I need to hear when in a downward spiral.

Of course, reading the Bible is crucial, as it is filled with truth and messages that apply to me. However, I've found that caution is still necessary as misinterpretation can quickly warp the meaning of a passage of scripture. That doesn't help me get to the truth at all. That's where backup plans like exercise and uplifting music come in handy. Later, I can revisit scripture with a clear mind and prevent the Enemy from further distorting what God is communicating to me in each passage.

Once I can sort through my thoughts, I often search for two specific things: attacks on my identity and attacks on my view of God. I ask myself, *What is this thought telling me?* All debilitating lies are the ones that impact my belief of who I am and who God is. If I do not see the connection to those, I have not dug deep enough.

We must also identify the truth. I know my lies so well that I often know the truths I need to counter them with. That's where a large part of my trust in God comes into play. I must trust that He will provide me with an opportunity to engage Him in the presence of those lies and embrace the truth once again. It does not have to always be challenges like entering a superstore or giving a speech. Sometimes it is the small things in life, like when I decided to vacuum at the house.

Putting away a vacuum may sound a bit absurd for a struggle. I still find myself chuckling at the simplicity of it when I remember the occasion. But it is a great example of an everyday activity in which I was able to engage God and a lie was overcome. That is the kind of thing to look for on a day-to-day basis. When I am diligent in noticing and handling the small things, I am more inclined to act appropriately when larger and more important issues arise.

THINGS TO THINK ABOUT

1) With so much going on in our lives, it's often easy to overlook the warning signs like those that I described, from anxiety to anger to hopelessness. What can you do to slow your life down and pay attention to your unique warning signs? Do you know the "prayer closets," or quiet corners of your life, that work best for you? If not, how might you overcome the barriers that prevent you from connecting with God and what's really going on in your life?

_____

_____

2) I have certain signs that manifest when I am giving in to a lie, many times unknowingly. Anxiety, anger, and hopelessness are the red flags that tell us something is wrong, but they can be difficult to catch if you do not recognize how you uniquely experience them. You might feel guilty all the time, struggle desperately to please others, keep yourself busy to an unhealthy level, clean excessively, be obsessed with specific eating habits, flirt a lot, engage in reckless behavior, try to prove yourself to others, or engage in a myriad of other possibilities. Take some time to identify your unique warning signs that prove you are actively believing a lie.

_____

_____

_____

3) I learned how to face my fears by consciously taking control of my thoughts and actively engaging my relationship with God. I also learned the importance of not just big events, but the everyday battles. That's where the most ground is gained or lost in a war, the oft-overlooked day-to-day life. How we treat those moments is where the truth can become truly cemented into us. Look at your list of personal lies that you fall victim to. Take the time to notice how they play a role in your life, especially in the last day or two. Do not be ashamed or afraid to explore what appears to be the smallest and most insignificant activities of your day.

_____

_____

_____

(16)

True Peace

I RUSH INTO THE HOUSE AND THROW MY STUFF FROM WORK ON THE COUNTER. Tonight is a very big night, and I do not want us to be late.

"Hey Dad," my son, Michael, says to me.

"Hey buddy, are you ready to go?" I know he's not. He's a last-minute kind of guy. He's never had the tendency to arrive at events early and over-prepared like me; not even for his own high school graduation.

"Almost, I just need to put on my clothes really quick. I need you to look at my bowtie and tell me if it's okay," he says.

"Alright, go get it on and I will take a look," I respond. I really do not understand the sudden fascination with bowties among Michael and his peers. If I wore something like that in high school, I would've been dumped in a trashcan and rolled down the hall. But now it's cool to wear them. Or fresh, groovy, or something like that. It's amazing how styles change over what feels like such a short time. The bowties do look good on him though.

After a while, he comes back downstairs, dressed and ready to go. I can tell that he has something on his mind as I work to straighten his tie. Unlike me, he is not good at hiding things. Another difference that I am thankful for! The harder it is for him to hide, the better. Flimsy masks encourage a person to more speedily face those difficult emotions in life like hurt, shame, and rejection.

Many choices Michael makes in life are the opposite of what I would choose, with only a few exceptions. For one, I love how he dresses himself. I choose more subtle and darker colors, so I don't stand out. In contrast, he chooses the bright colors, so that he stands out as much as possible. He is an extrovert, finding much of his energy in being around people. I am charged up by being alone. He waits to the last minute on things, and he is very spontaneous and fun, always looking for the next adventure. I, on the other hand, plan way ahead of time what I am going to do. Spontaneity does not come naturally for me. Truth be told, much of what I know about spontaneity has come from Michael.

Finally, he says something about what is on his mind. "I have something for you." He runs to get something from his room.

All I can guess is that he has some sort of gift for me. Although he often appears sporadic in his thinking, he is quite thoughtful.

He returns quickly from his room, visibly excited to give me a folded piece of paper. Through the paper I can read the words "Dear Dad" at the top. I know immediately that this will not be an easy read without shedding some tears. When he shares his heart, Michael does not hold back. That is another difference between him and me. He is uninhibited when it comes to sharing his heart. I cannot read this letter with both him and his girlfriend present to witness my reaction.

"Thank you, son. I will go read this and get ready to go, okay?" He nods. I go to the bedroom to read it alone.

The letter has quite a bit in it. As I anticipated, the paper is covered with a veritable flood of emotions. On this treasured note, he addresses much about our relationship from accepting my imperfections as his father to apologizing for his own shortcomings. I cannot believe how well he encapsulates our relationship in its entirety with just three-quarters of a page. As I read, my desire to hurry and my worry about being late melts away. Nothing is more important than this letter right now.

One part of this letter catches my attention. After his sharing of gratitude and love for me, he ends this letter with a sentence that will stay with me for a long time:

Whoever doubted you in the past, you sure proved them wrong, Dad.

God is speaking directly through my own son, validating me once more. I revel in the feeling this brings. I can never have enough of it. He knows that, which is why He sneaks these things in from time to time. But coming from my son, this only serves to establish further the long journey that's been made and the trials that have been overcome to reach this point. And it feels good.

Yes son, those doubts, fears, and lies most certainly have been proven wrong.

❖ A FATHER'S AFFECTION ❖

I am sure Michael has wondered why he is so different than me at times. Did he ever recognize the differences and worry about it? Did he think he wasn't measuring up to my expectations because of how dissimilar we are? I ponder these questions because I know what it feels like to believe I do not measure up somehow. I know what it's like to live my life believing I am too different, weird, or messed up to be accepted. I know what it's like to believe that nothing I do is pleasing to my Father. I know what it's like to constantly think I am a failure due to my imperfections. I also know the personal consequences of believing such things. Things like fear, anxiety and panic attacks eventually become all-consuming. I've never wanted for my son to go through a day thinking he was unloved. I'm sure God never wanted it for me either.

Like me, Michael wasn't always a perfect son. However, his imperfections have made it possible for me to love him even more deeply. Loving someone who does everything you want them to do is easy. Loving someone who strays from the decisions you want them to make is a whole different ballgame. It takes grace and true love to care for someone in the midst of their making mistakes. This has served greatly as a glimpse of how God the Father loves me, one of His sons.

I've had many temptations to withhold my love from my son, due to disagreements and fights over the years. I know I've goofed many times as a parent. Withholding love is never an acceptable punishment. Not only that, the result is fruitless. It never manipulates anyone into making positive changes. Paul was right when he told the Corinthians speaking to others without love is like a clanging cymbal (1 Corinthians 13:1). It's annoying and it hurts. Relationships shatter in the absence of love, and without relationships, what do we really have left?

In my relationship with my son, I've found in him a reflection of how God views me. My son cannot do anything that will change the fact that he is my son. His place in my heart is safe and secure no matter how many mistakes he makes along the way. Likewise, even in my most imperfect moment, God's affections toward me have always remained steadfast and constant. He has never withheld his love from me, not as punishment or even as some sneaky form of manipulation.

Loving Neil McLamb required a lot on God's part. The death of His son was required to overcome the hurdle of proving His love to me and to help bring me back into His presence. His Grace has washed away every conceivable doubt I could throw at Him. A lifetime of trying to please Him with "good deeds" could never match the overwhelming realization that He loves me no matter what I do. I hope and pray that my son has caught a glimpse of that love. It's all he really needs.

I did not share everything with Michael that I've endured through the years, especially during the most difficult portions of my journey. However, I definitely put effort into sharing some of my struggles with him, particularly when I saw him struggling with similar issues. The statement he ended his letter with still shocks me, as I had no idea he realized the ongoing struggle with fear and doubt that plagued me for so long.

From the time that I was just a little boy, pushing myself not to cry when my parents left me for my first day in kindergarten, until I stepped into that superstore, the voices of doubt were loud and clear. I projected my own insecurities onto those around me. I believed that everyone around me saw something wrong when they looked at me. Even worse, I perceived that God held the same belief.

My son was right. The lies and doubt that held me prisoner for so many years have been proven wrong. Those beliefs that I projected onto others did not stand up to the truth once I discovered it and began living it. I may falter from time to time and allow the lies to creep back in, bringing back the doubt, but thanks to many years of experiencing the truth in my life, I know how to fight back. Now I can prove them wrong once again, and move forward in the truth about who I truly am: significant, accepted, secure, and above all else… loved.

With many fears present—which life has not stopped throwing them at me—knowing the truth and how to live in it pays off greatly. Financial concerns, change, showing emotion, letting Michael move into new stages in life, and the inevitable "empty nest" my wife and I are now facing are all things that stir up old lies, provoking past fears that threaten to take hold of me again. Heck, even knowing I would be asked to pray in front of people to bless the food at Michael's graduation party was a challenge. Public speaking will, no doubt, always be an opportunity to take a step of faith. Typically, it's a hard one, but always seems to end in rewarding ways.

In the midst of all these trials and blessings, I have found what I have been looking for all along:

Peace.

I settled for false versions of it several times. One of them was called "I don't care." Another was when I attempted perfection in my course work during graduate school. Another I sought through the attention of girls. Substance abuse was yet another. The list goes on and on. What I sought all along was peace, but I mistook many imposters in life for the real thing, until I finally found it. True peace is found only when we face our fears instead of running from them.

I realized there was a problem when the symptoms of anxiety, and then panic attacks, plagued me. I tried to control it all by avoiding the underlying causes for as long as I could, much of the time out of ignorance. After suffering for what felt like an eternity, I reached a point when I could, at last... surrender to all that was beyond my control. I discovered what was leading to all the symptoms. I uncovered many lies that contributed toward my troublesome behaviors and feelings. When I finally began to address the root cause of these symptoms, I developed hope. It was hope I found in the truth that gave me the strength to push forward to the next stage of my struggle.

There's a passage in scripture (Proverbs 9:10, ESV) that says "The fear of the LORD is the beginning of wisdom, and the knowledge of the Holy One is insight." My experiences have taught me how true this is. Though the anxiety and panic attacks were products of lies, fear actually contributed toward me finding the truth. The anxiety acted as warning lights on the dashboard of my car. Something was wrong, very wrong. Without His truth, there are many things to fear! The absence of truth leaves you subject only to lies that torment and threaten to destroy you.

As I dug deeper, I realized how my fears all led to God in some way. Sure, most were unhealthy and built on lies, but that fear brought me to a point where I became humble enough to desire the truth. The knowledge I acquired during that stage of my journey was crucial. It revealed the lies for what they were. It gave me ammo for the fights ahead. The truth compelled me to finally face my fears.

Knowledge is not enough. As powerful as it is, knowledge does not carry us through to the end of our journey with fear. I can know a lot about anything, but experiencing it is a different thing altogether. I may know a lot of stuff about my wife and son, but loving them and being loved by them brings life to the knowledge I already have. There is no comparison. The love found in a relationship makes the knowledge a reality. Love is the last revelation on the journey. It is the foundation upon which all other things in life can be built. It brings relevance to the meaning of true life, instead of mere existence. It gives us motivation to press forward. In fact, it propels us forward to succeed. It helps us find strength, understanding, and freedom. The true peace we need is always found in our Father's Grace. When we see ourselves the way He sees us, we do not live in fear. In the presence of God's unconditional love, fear loses its power and our shame melts away.

During this time of transition, I can no longer view my son as a young boy whom I can keep under my roof and protection. Now I must embrace him as a young man moving on to make his own path in finding his own name. I could worry about how many times I have messed up with Michael and the impact it's had on him. I could focus on how my time with him as a boy is over and I can't have any do-overs. I could continuously worry about his future choices and experiences and allow the fear to take over.

Thankfully, that's not my only option. Living in truth and the reality of being loved is a better option, because it offers something more in life than sitting back and being "okay" with everything that's happening. It offers more than merely living in survival mode. It offers joy and freedom in life instead of the hardship of trying to maintain control. It also gives the ability to share this powerful love with others. I need love. My family needs it. We all need it.

We do not have to continue living in the midst of fear. We are not alone. God is there with us, beckoning us into His powerful truth and unconditional love.

THINGS TO THINK ABOUT

There were seven identifiable stages in my journey:

<u>Fear and Shame</u>: I did and experienced things that led to being ashamed and afraid. I learned to avoid things I was afraid of and hid my shame. I tried various ways of giving up and trying harder. I did not see any of this as a problem.

<u>Symptoms</u>: I began to have symptoms of anxiety and then panic attacks. These symptoms made me aware that there was a problem. Other periodic symptoms in my life were things like anger and feelings of hopelessness.

<u>Surrender</u>: After fighting to maintain control until I was utterly exhausted, I chose to surrender my efforts to control my fears and my symptoms.

<u>Beliefs</u>: I learned there was a problem with what I believed about God and myself that led directly to the symptoms I was experiencing. I believed many lies and lived as if they were true. I finally discovered the truths that gave me hope, and those became knowledge I could use against the lies.

<u>Faith</u>: The truth compelled me to begin questioning the lies and facing my fears. I learned how to trust God and put my faith into action.

<u>Love</u>: I realized something was missing and relied on God to provide the final puzzle piece to make it all come together for me, resulting in experiencing His love in a new and life changing way. I learned to embrace this love as an unconditional gift I did not have to be perfect to receive.

<u>Peace</u>: True peace comes from embracing and residing in our Father's Grace, unconditionally loved and free of any masks we may have conjured up along the way. Through experiencing His Grace, I continue to learn how to live this life of "being loved," all while applying the truth and facing fears along the way with God right beside me.

1) Which one of these stages do you see yourself at in your own journey? Perhaps your experiences are a bit different than mine, but you can find yourself in one of these stages.

_____

_____

2) What do you see as your next step of faith? Is it acknowledging the signs and symptoms in your life that something is wrong? Is it coming to that very difficult decision to surrender control? Do you need to discover the lies you believe? Is it time to face your first big fear? Are you waiting on God for an answer to a big question you have about who you are or who He really is?

_____

_____

3) Every single step of my journey has been important as God used each one to lead me out of the bondages of fear and shame. However, the most precious and life-changing part has been experiencing His grace and the never-ending love He has for me. It is something I find a need to embrace each and every day of my life. Regardless of what "stage" you might be in, spend time opening yourself up to and seeking this love the Father has for you. We never can get enough of it, and it changes everything.

_____

_____

Afterword

Neil never battled anxiety again in his life.

He went on to climb Mt. Everest. He discovered a previously unknown galaxy. In his free time he digs wells for impoverished villages with his bare hands. His family has gone on to be more attractive, more wealthy, and more healthy than other families. He is always at peace with himself while at the same time striving for ever greater advancement in life.

Well, not exactly.

It's actually much better than that.

As a friend, I've been able to watch Neil handle his daily life with courage and humility. Anxiety can sometimes reappear, but he addresses it using the lessons he's learned over the past few years. He has graciously shared those lessons with you in this book. Understanding and accepting life as a process is the key to emotional and spiritual health. There are good days and bad. Those who succeed embrace the good days and refuse to allow bad days to define them. Neil does that better than anyone I know.

I hope that you've found hope in these pages. If you have, I hope you'll share this book with a friend or someone in your family. Anxiety can be miserable in and of itself, but it's unbearable if you face it alone. I also hope that you have been inspired by Neil's story as much as I have, and that it will give you the courage to start your own journey from *Panic to Peace*.

Michael Ramsey, Ph.D.

Acknowledgements

I would like to thank my wife, Melissa, for her unending love and support throughout the process of writing and everything else that went into the completion of this book. I would also like to thank my son Michael for his understanding and support as I devoted time to the tasks involved in finishing the book, as well as him unknowingly contributing so much to the last chapter with his love and encouragement through a letter.

To my parents, Michael and Gaile, I was no doubt a difficult child to figure out. I was a master hider. Thank you for not giving up on me and loving me regardless.

I also thank Adam, Lauren, Poppie, Mama T., Granddaddy, Estalene, Marsha, Daniel, Jessica, Jennifer, and the rest of my family. You all have loved and supported me throughout the years. I cannot express enough how much of a blessing you all are to me. My story would not be complete without all of you.

Michael R., Jennifer B., and Lizzie…words cannot express the gratitude I have for the hours you spent offering suggestions, edits, and a host of other contributions that made this book better than it could have ever been without you.

Michael R., much of the story in this book hinged on your involvement in my life. For offering your time and love at one of the most crucial time periods I have experienced, I can never thank you enough.

Johnny, your care and insight was very helpful to me during an important part of my life that was covered in this book. I am very grateful that God brought us together.

I offer a special thank you to a very talented editor, Ryan. You took a very rough manuscript, cleaned it up, wrestled with me on some important things, and inevitably helped to transform what had been written into what it is now. If the readers could only see that first rough manuscript that you received from me, they would send you their gratitude as well!

Kevin, thanks for the cover art you provided to frame my story. I needed a gifted heart and mind like yours to create something I could never have dreamed up myself. It fits the story perfectly, and I could not be more pleased with it.

A sincere thanks goes to Lavelle, Melanie, Daniel, Jennifer A., Beth, Scott, Tony, and Janet who provided special insight along the way, as I was putting everything together to make this book a reality.

I am appreciative to a Father who loves me relentlessly. The story I have shared was truly a difficult journey. However, God walked patiently with me throughout the whole thing, loving me, teaching me, and encouraging me along the way. He still does today, as my story is not quite finished.

About the Author

Neil McLamb has been married to his wife, Melissa, since 1997. Since then, they have resided in a small community in Sampson County, NC, near where they both grew up. They have one son, Michael, who recently moved out to attend college. Melissa is a nurse practitioner and has a passion for helping others back to health. Michael is the extrovert who is energized by being around people. God has worked through him for years to pull Neil and Melissa out of their introverted shells.

Neil finished college with an MBA and worked as an accountant for several years before facing his struggle with anxiety and panic attacks. During and after that period of time, he served as a Youth Minister, was ordained as a minister, and earned master and doctoral degrees in counseling. He has since enjoyed meeting many people along the way and serving them as their counselor.

Neil enjoys sharing his own story with others, through his writing and in person. He loves how God works to heal and grow both the people he connects with, as well as himself. Exploring, experiencing, and sharing God's Grace is a central part of what he does. He enjoys helping others discover and learn how to act on faith in order to experience the true freedom God offers through Christ.

http://www.neilmclamb.com
http://www.facebook.com/drneilmclamb
http://twitter.com/neilmclamb